READINGS IN GERONTOLOGY

READINGS IN GERONTOLOGY

Edited by

MOLLIE BROWN, R.S.M., R.N., Ph.D. (candidate)

Director, Ambulatory Service
Genesee Mental Health Center
Rochester, New York

SECOND EDITION

THE C. V. MOSBY COMPANY

Saint Louis   1978

SECOND EDITION

Copyright © 1978 by The C. V. Mosby Company

All rights reserved. No part of this book may be reproduced in any manner without written permission of the publisher.

Previous edition copyrighted 1973

Printed in the United States of America
Distributed in Great Britain by Henry Kimpton, London

The C. V. Mosby Company
11830 Westline Industrial Drive, St. Louis, Missouri 63141

Library of Congress Cataloging in Publication Data

Main entry under title:

Readings in gerontology.

    First ed. (1973) by V. M. Brantl and M. R. Brown.
    Includes bibliographies.
    1. Gerontology—Addresses, essays, lectures.
2. Geriatrics—Addresses, essays, lectures. I. Brown,
Mollie, 1931-   II. Brantl, Virginia M., 1925-1975
comp. Readings in gerontology. [DNLM: 1. Geriatrics—
Collected works. WT5 R287]
HQ1061.R363 1978   618.9′7′008   77-14088
ISBN 0-8016-0734-5

GW/M/M 9 8 7 6 5 4 3 2 1

FOREWORD

Gerontology, the study of aging, is a relatively new area of scientific inquiry. With increasing numbers of older persons in the population, major issues in regard to our social policies and practices toward the aging have arisen. The phenomenon of aging has had a major impact on our social arrangements and institutions, including the family, government, and the political process and income maintenance and work, as well as in the areas of health and social welfare delivery systems.

The application of knowledge to human aging requires multidisciplinary focus. Thus for those who would develop programs of services or who would prepare persons to work with older people, there is need for an interdisciplinary approach. In addition, there is an interdependence among practice, training, and research. Those who would work with older persons must have, in addition to humanistic values and skills, knowledge of the theories of aging—biological, sociological, and psychological—the relevant research in these areas, and a view as to how such theories and research findings may be applied through practice. There is a further need for training practitioners in needed skills as well as perspectives for a new generation of practitioners in the health, social, and rehabilitative professions. Finally, practitioners must learn to identify and organize the data and social facts that grow out of practice and relate these to the university and research laboratories so that research may raise the right questions and develop new perspectives regarding the social usefulness of such research.

Through the perceptive editorship of Dr. Virginia M. Brantl and Sister Marie Raymond Brown, this set of readings has been organized to provide the reader with an understanding of the relationship between theory, research, and practice. Included are papers presenting some of the "cutting edges" of gerontology. Having these writings organized under one cover should be useful to the practitioner, the teacher, and the student.

There is, indeed, a need to develop commitments to and identities with the aging among the young, the educators, and those seeking middle careers. Due to our cultural and social biases, there is a shortage of curriculum offerings in gerontology in our universities and colleges and vast shortages in trained manpower to work toward meeting the varied needs of our approximately 21 million persons over 65 years of age. This book of readings should help to develop such commitments by pointing the way, through concepts and knowledge of the status of research and some of the major issues in gerontology. Furthermore, it should serve as a bridge between knowledge and practice concerning some of the major issues confronting older persons.

Walter M. Beattie, Jr.

Director, All-University Gerontology Center,
Syracuse University, Syracuse, New York

PREFACE to second edition

In 1972, Dr. Virginia Brantl and I decided to edit a book of articles drawn from the gerontological and behavioral science literature. The first edition was well received by those working directly and indirectly with older people.

Three years later, The C. V. Mosby Company asked us to consider a revision of that work, including some original chapters. We were delighted with the request and began planning. In August of 1975, Dr. Brantl died very unexpectedly.

There are four original chapters in this edition. Dr. Jacquelyne J. Jackson and Dr. Bertram E. Walls, both of the Center for the Study of Aging and Human Development at Duke University, have co-authored a chapter on the myths and realities about the black aged in American society. Nancy Fugate Woods, also of Duke University, has expanded a section of her work on human sexuality in health and illness to a full chapter on human sexuality in the well elderly. I have added two companion chapters that address themselves to the intergenerational relationships of two groups of elderly and their children and to a beginning conceptualization of the developmental tasks of these two older groups.

This revision has been a pleasant task for me. It has provided both the impetus and the vehicle for my early thinking on the separate developmental tasks of two distinct groups of elderly. More than this, however, it has been the fulfillment of a promise and, as such, it is dedicated to the memory of a dear friend and colleague, Dr. Virginia Brantl.

Mollie Brown

PREFACE to first edition

Older persons in our society have in a sense been pioneers in that advances in technology and health care have enhanced the chances of living to an age that only a few generations ago would have been the exception to the rule. Since the effects of the aging process are not uniform, there also seems to be no way to determine the sequence of study of these phenomena. Hence a continual search for comprehensive theories and their application is vital so that we may understand the complexities of the forces at work in this phase of the life span.

Whereas increasing numbers of monographs, articles, and reading texts have been devoted to the problems of our aging population, numerous other concepts and empirical findings related to the psychological, physiological, and sociological aspects of the lives of our elderly citizens have appeared in a highly fragmented fashion in the literature. Because of the nature of this isolation of the reportable data, for this book we chose to select readings that would tie together underlying concepts and principles directed toward a multidisciplinary approach to the study of the aged. No attempt has been made, however, to cover any of these contributions comprehensively, since in time these selections could be added to or modified as our understanding of the aging process becomes more accurate and predictable.

The aim of this book of readings, therefore, was to select a systematic ordering of the most recent and relevant issues, which, it is hoped, will generate further research and implementation of theories in those disciplines related to the field of gerontology. This volume has the advantage of containing a variety of sources representative of the disciplines of gerontology, psychology, physiology, medical science, sociology, social work, genetics, and nutrition.

We wish to express our sincere gratitude and appreciation to our contributors for granting us permission to reproduce their ideas and suggestions. We wish also to acknowledge the many people who have been of assistance to us in the preparation of this book. Sister Mary Clare Bollow, acting as secretary to the editors, handled all correspondence with the publishers and authors and maintained records. Her assistance was invaluable. Mrs. Lucretia McClure of the Edward G. Miner Library at the University of Rochester Medical Center and Mrs. Ruby Smith, Reference Librarian at the Milton Hershey Medical Center of the Pennsylvania State University, were untiring in their search of the literature and their offers of technical assistance.

Walter M. Beattie, Jr., Director of the All-University Gerontology Center at Syracuse University and formerly Dean of the School of Social Work at Syracuse, kindly agreed to write the foreword for this book. Much of the motivation and momentum for this work was due to the workshops on gerontology that Walter Beattie led during 1970-1972. Mrs. Dorothy Johnson, Project Director for those workshops, was also responsible for initiating our interest in preparing such an anthology.

Virginia M. Brantl
Sister Marie Raymond Brown

CONTENTS

READINGS IN GERONTOLOGY

THE NEW AGED: THE YOUNG-OLD AND THE VULNERABLE OLD

Mollie Brown, R.S.M., R.N., Ph.D. (candidate)

One of the strongest, most enduring values of American society is its support of the individuality of its citizens. From the earliest days of the frontier, the image of the solitary horseman riding off into the sunset has become the symbol of the independent individual, carving out a place in society.

The value of the individual, ingrained in children by parents and teachers, is rewarded at all levels of the culture. How ironic, then, at old age, the zenith of individuality, that the same society has fallen into the lumping syndrome of assigning all older citizens to the category of "65 and over." At a time of life when the most highly differentiated coping patterns have been developed, the elderly are consigned to a homogenized whole, losing any individuality they had attained in their lives.

This chapter is an attempt to identify some of the unique characteristics of older Americans. One way of conceptualizing the differences among the elderly (those 65 or over, as defined by Social Security and Medicare) is to describe them as different cohorts and plot those cohorts against a historical time line, much the way Bühler (1962) describes her psychohistorical approach to life.

Fig. 1 offers a graphic overview of several generations of Americans. The horizontal axis represents a rather broadly spaced time line against which are plotted some of the major events that have touched the lives of most Americans.

This discussion will deal mainly with cohorts A and B. However, it is important to place these two cohorts within the context of the other generations, since many of the attitudes and socioeconomic decisions that are formed and implemented are shaped by cohorts C and D. Moreover, even though this chapter deals specifically with the young-old and the vulnerable old, the decisions made by the middle generation and its adult children affect both ends of the continuum.

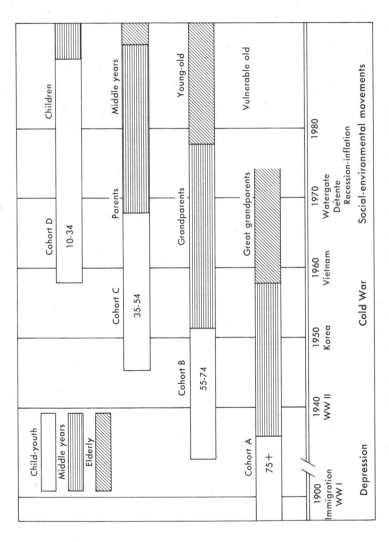

Fig. 1. Historical overview of intergenerational families in American society.

Before proceeding to the body of the discussion, the two terms *young-old* and *vulnerable old* need to be clarified. During 1972 and 1973, the Sloan Foundation funded research in selected universities across the country. Its mandate was to develop a multidisciplinary approach to formulating social policy for the elderly.

The University of Chicago group found it necessary to distinguish between the young-old and the old-old, since the social policy needs and implications for these two groups were seen as qualitatively different. Using arbitrary ages, the Chicago group identified the young-old as ranging from 55 to 74 years of age. Phenomena such as early voluntary retirement and better physical health seemed to distinguish this group from the old-old, those 75 and over.

In this chapter, I choose to refer to the younger of these two groups (cohort B) as the *young-old,* those still physically healthy, independent, and able to manipulate many of the social systems they participate in. The term *vulnerable old* is used to refer to the older group (cohort A) and implies that, although many are still healthy and independent, people in this cohort are more vulnerable to physical, social, and psychological assaults on their person by virtue of the physiological changes they endure in the aging process.

THE VULNERABLE OLD: GREAT GRANDPARENTS

Immigration, that wrenching away from the rich ethnic and cultural roots of a people, may well have been one of the first major experiences of the vulnerable old, those people who are now in their late seventies, eighties, and beyond. For some of that generation, immigrating to this country may have been their own decision, a hope for freedom and a better future. For others, it may have been a parental decision over which they had no control, but for whom it was an exciting, perhaps frightening experience.

If European immigrants of this generation were lucky, they arrived at Ellis Island or elsewhere on the east coast of America and moved into an already established ethnic neighborhood. In an eagerness to blend and obtain jobs, many of this cohort's practices were submerged, denied, negated. Although the parents may never have learned to speak English well, their children did. This was an important and necessary move, but it was the first of many losses the parental generation was to face.

If the children of this generation were old enough, they went to fight in a "war to end war." Here was another trauma for the vulnerable old. Not only were their sons going off to war and its concomitant dangers, but those same sons might well be in combat with relatives and friends who chose to stay in the old country.

This generation (cohort A) was the first to live through the Depression as adults. Although their children (cohort B) felt the Depression by going without luxuries and sometimes necessities, they were not faced with making painful decisions. It was the parental generation that had to decide whether families were to split up and children placed with relatives to be fed and clothed.

The vulnerable old will say, without hesitation, that theirs was a harder lot. To have to make decisions that affected one's children was a much more difficult task than was the children's living out of the decision. One 82-year-old remarked that she still wondered whether her and her husband's decision to place some of their children with relatives during the Depression had any influence on these children's subsequent marital difficulties.

With the coming of the 1940s and the nationwide gearing up for World War II, the Depression generation and their children moved into a spiraling economy that was to continue for almost two decades.

The generation known as the vulnerable old have lived through two world wars, a police action in Korea, the Cold War, and Vietnam. At home, they lived through the Depression, a spiraling inflation, recessions, détentes, and social revolutions. They learned to cope with these events as well as more intensely personal ones—illness, death, crippling disease—with varying degrees of mastery.

The vulnerable old have lived long enough to see the cycle of history begin to repeat itself. For them, the recession and stock-market losses of the 1970s were highly reminiscent of 1929. Unless the federal government is careful, its nutrition program for the elderly and its food stamp program, which are meant to help people in need, may also seem highly reminiscent of the soup and bread lines of those earlier days.

This generation of Americans, many of whom were immigrants or children of immigrants, considered themselves fortunate to have completed eighth grade; 72% of them did so. Because of this low level of education, language barriers, and the sequential waves of immigration, the vulnerable old held low-skilled, low-paying jobs. Those who worked on the railroad had fair pensions, but the majority of cohort A moved into their late sixties with minimal pension benefits and relatively low Social Security rates. Multiple losses through the years, the natural losses of the physiological aging process, and the stresses accompanying a lifetime of hard work have brought this cohort to a time in their lives when the majority are dependent on their kin or strangers for many of the necessities of life.

A generation who valued their independence and stamina now find themselves highly vulnerable to the pace of the late 1970s. For every 82-year-old who comes independently to a federal nutrition site and claims that "It is only by standing together that we will be heard," there are many others who are isolated and lonely in their own small dwellings or in institutions. Although it is true that at any one time only 7% to 9% of the elderly are in institutions (hospitals or nursing and proprietary homes), a majority of that 7% to 9% is 82 and older.

The preceding discussion of the vulnerable old (*cohort A* in Fig. 1) has perhaps presented a depressing view of them. It is important, however, that the reader not fall into the easy stereotyping of the lumping syndrome. There are many aged people in society who are deeply involved with their peers in highly satisfying activities, such as church groups and the Gray Panthers. It is important to remember that the vulnerable old, although admittedly vulnerable—physically, socially, and psychologically—are also an independent breed of men and women for whom it has been and continues to be difficult to learn how to be dependent again without losing their self-respect.

THE YOUNG-OLD: GRANDPARENTS

The cohort of the young-old (*B* in Fig. 1) is also a highly individual group with its own historical perspective. The majority of this age group are first-generation Americans. Some came to America with their immigrant parents and soon were Americanized into their neighborhoods and social institutions. Although they, too, lived through the Great Depression, they more often felt the effects of decisions made by their parents rather than having to make those decisions themselves.

Educationally they forged ahead of their parents. Almost 50% of this generation completed high school or its equivalent, whereas 72% of their parents had completed only the equivalent of an eighth-grade education. This statistic alone is an important factor in this group's economic standard of living. The young-old became the generation who worked in the wartime economy of the 1940s and 1950s. By this time labor was becoming a strong political force, and working conditions were vastly improved. The Social Security system was in operation, and workers began to have a sense that their later years would be economically comfortable.

This cohort tended to marry earlier than did their parents of the Depression; they had more children, and they had them earlier. Hence, by the time they were in their middle years, their children (cohort C) were in high school and college. This generation also managed to do what their parents had done and gave their children more educational benefits.

Socially and economically, this generation of young-old had learned to manipulate many of the systems that the economy had created. They were actively involved in their labor unions. They were the generation with the highest voting record and so were a political force to be reckoned with.

Because of their higher educational level, they were able to hold better jobs than their parents had and so had more discretionary dollars to use in establishing their life-styles. Although their experiences with the Depression era were still part of their life histories, the ever-spiraling economy gave them a sound base from which to travel, to think about early retirement plans, and to toy with the idea of second careers. Their parents were locked into one work life because of educational and economic constraints, but this group of the young-old could think about changing careers, and in many cases they did so.

The implications of this cohort's history will be broadly felt in the future. This generation of young-old will make more demands on the political, economic, and social systems. They will exact increases in Social Security benefits to help offset the rising cost of living. Their health concerns will include a more preventive orientation. They will avail themselves of continuing educational opportunities in their communities and request courses to answer specific needs. They will need counseling services to help them find meaning in life and meaningful relationships in their later years.

THE MIDDLE YEARS: PARENTS

Although this chapter deals with the vulnerable old and the young-old, it is necessary to discuss briefly the generation of the middle years. This group of 35- to 55-year-olds is a powerful force in society. They are at the peak of their earning potential; they tend to vote regularly and are involved in civic and neighborhood responsibilities. Because of these characteristics, this cohort makes decisions that deeply affect cohorts A and B. The wage base for Social Security taxes is measured on their earnings. Neighborhood safety for their children and the care of elderly relatives are some of the boundaries of their interests. They want their children safe; they want their parents cared for adequately. But members of this same cohort find themselves torn when they have to make choices about the future of their children and the future of their elders. Do they put their money into providing more for their children, or do they direct more money into services for the elderly? The choice is difficult when funds are limited.

This chapter is primarily a discussion of the two different cohorts of older Americans. Therefore, although there is a wealth of information on the other cohorts contained in Fig. 1, those data and their implications will not be discussed further.

However, it is important that this discussion of older Americans not stop with a description of their lifelines. There are important implications for both basic research with the elderly and the applied professions that deal with the older generations.

IMPLICATIONS

Researchers who work with the elderly and with intergenerational families can no longer lump the older generation into "those over 65." Even though multiple data are collected in this manner, the difference between cohorts must be teased out if hypotheses are to be tested carefully and generalizations made from these findings. Gerontologists and students of gerontology must make themselves acutely aware of the many variables that impinge on the study of the vulnerable old and the young-old.

It is equally imperative that members of the applied professions—medicine, social work, nursing, law, religion—make themselves aware of the wide range of individuality in the two elderly generations in American society. For instance, as mentioned earlier, great care must be observed in the operation of the federal nutrition programs. The vulnerable old, many of whom are still living independently in their own homes or in senior citizen settings, are able to participate in the nutrition program. They must not be reminded of an earlier era of the 1930s, when they and their children stood in soup and bread lines to get enough nourishment. The potential for multiple services to be located in their nutrition centers would do much to make those services special for the elderly.

If Medicare and Medicaid are to be of real value to the elderly, those programs must be reasonably available to all older Americans. In reality two classes of health care have evolved: the public sector, stringently controlled by utilization review and placement programs, and the private sector, where financially-able elderly have several options from which to choose. For instance, in many sections of the country there are proprietary homes that will not accept SSI* recipients and nursing homes that will not accept Medicaid patients because those programs do not pay enough to make it feasible for these institutions to maintain such individuals.

There is, at the present time, no simple method of taking care of the older person who, although not declared incompetent, is in fact unable to care for himself. Conservatorships can be appointed by the courts to care for real property and since 1975 can now be extended to care for the elderly confused individual who no longer can care for himself. Such a conservator could cash and deposit checks and do the other things the individual is no longer capable of doing for himself.

Churches, too, must begin to respond to the needs of their older members. Cohorts A and B were deeply involved in their religions. The church was for them a real source of comfort and strength in difficult times. These same cohorts were used to tithing and were committed to the financial support of their churches.

There is a significant proportion of the elderly who can no longer tithe or in other ways support their churches. Many of them choose not to attend church services because they cannot contribute to the support of the church. This decision, made at a time when older people need the spiritual and social support of religion, seems to demand that organized religions reexamine their priorities of pastoral care and deliberately direct more of their pastoral services to their older members.

Physicians, nurses, and other members of the health care system need to continue their recent approaches to viewing the elderly as individuals with distinct physiological and psychological needs. It is no longer possible to defend the statement that aches and pains are to be expected because one is old. Elderly people are susceptible to the same diseases as younger persons but are far more vulnerable to those diseases and their complications. The older human body responds differently to medications and combinations of medications. Younger patients ordinarily metabolize medications rapidly, whereas older patients tend to store medications in fat cells; hence medications reach toxic levels in their

---

*Supplemental Security Income, administered by the Social Security Administration.

bodies more quickly. Qualitative differences exist in vulnerable old individuals as compared to the young-old, and these must be recognized by care providers.

The discussion of implications in this distinction between the young-old and the vulnerable old could continue indefinitely. What is important here is that the reader make a conscious effort to become aware of the qualitative differences in the two groups of elderly.

If individuality is to continue to be a value in American society, it must extend to all of that society's citizens. Beginning with the elderly themselves and extending to all areas of social and economic life, people must continue to make themselves aware of the individuality of the elderly and approach them accordingly.

It is never sufficient for society to categorize its members in large groups and ignore individual differences. This society and those who implement its policies must do all in their power to identify needs and respond to them in a manner befitting the qualities of the elderly.

REFERENCES

Berkowitz, Morris, Ph.D. To age or not to age. A study of aging in downtown Niagara Falls. Niagara Falls, Ont.: 1976 (unpublished).

Bühler, Charlotte. Genetic aspects of the self. *Annals of the New York Academy of Sciences,* January 27, 1962, **96,**730-764.

Butler, Robert. *Why survive? Being old in America.* New York: Harper & Row, Publishers, 1975.

Fleming, Jon H. The aging in American society. A commentary on social and personal relationships. In Fields, W. S. (Ed.). *The aging person in America. Neurological and sensory disorders in the elderly.* New York: Grune & Stratton, 1975.

Havighurst, Robert. *Human development and education.* (Rev. ed.). New York: David McKay Co., Inc., 1973.

Maddox, George L. (Ed.). *The future of aging and the aged.* Atlanta: Southern Newspaper Publishers Association Foundation, 1972.

Manney, James D., Jr. *Aging in American society. An examination of concepts and issues.* Ann Arbor, Mich.: The Institute of Gerontology, The University of Michigan–Wayne State University, 1975.

Neugarten, Bernice L. (Ed.). Aging in the year 2000: a look at the future. Part II. *Gerontologist,* February, 1975, **25,** 1.

Riley, N. W., Johnson, N., and Foner, A. *Aging and society.* Vol. I. New York: Russell Sage Foundation, 1968.

Rosow, Irving. The social context of the aging. *Gerontologist,* 1973, **13**(1), 82-87.

Twente, Esther E. *Never too old. The aged in community life.* San Francisco: Jossey-Bass, Inc., Publishers, 1970.

University of Chicago Task Force. *Older people in 1990: social policy issues.* Report prepared for Sloan Foundation. Chicago, June, 1973 (unpublished).

U.S. Department of Health, Education, and Welfare, Office of Human Development, Administration on Aging. *Older Americans Act of 1965, as amended, and related acts.* Washington, D.C., March, 1976.

DEVELOPMENTAL TASKS
OF TWO COHORTS OF ELDERLY:
A BEGINNING EXPLORATION

Mollie Brown, R.S.M., R.N., Ph.D. (candidate)

The concept of developmental tasks began early in the 1950s with Erikson's *Childhood and Society* and the "eight stages of man." Erikson began the conceptual development of stages in the life cycle, and he essentially set up polarities that characterized each stage. If one were to achieve the positive tasks successfully, one could approach the next stage of growth with a pattern of success.

Later in the same decade, Havighurst published his first edition of *Developmental Tasks and Education*. Based on the Eriksonian concept of developmental stages in growth, Havighurst began spelling out some specific tasks that one needed to accomplish to achieve the positive pole of each of the stages. Like most educators, Havighurst concentrated on ages that were part of the school-age population. Unlike most educators, however, he did attempt to spell out the developmental tasks of young adults, those in their middle years, and those 60 and older.

It is this last group that is the main concern of this chapter. In recent years there has been increasing emphasis on the study of the older population. There is a beginning move to see the elderly more as individuals with specific age-developmental needs rather than as a chronological category of people 65 years and older.

The history of age 65 began with the New Deal and the development of the Social Security Administration. An arbitrary age was set at which people could

I wish to express my gratitude to Robert Havighurst and Bernice Neugarten for their careful and critical reactions to this conceptual model.

begin to receive their additional support from taxes they had paid. Because of this, and partly because the labor market needed to make room for younger workers, this arbitrary age of 65 was also set for retirement from most work roles.

Because America was essentially a production society, those 65 and older began to be viewed as old and unable to make decisions about many parts of their lives, ranging from living arrangements to health care. New social programs such as Medicare began to operate on the same arbitrary age scale to help care for nonproductive citizens.

Because individuals tend to respond to the expectations placed on them, the elderly began to respond to the expectations of inability to make decisions, to retire from all activity (not just job-related activities), and to become willing to assume the passive roleless role in a production-oriented society. The above statements are true of many of the elderly, but it is also true that there are some elderly who, as Dylan Thomas pleaded, will not "go gentle into that good night." These are the Garson Meyers and Maggie Kuhns of this country. Older people who are like the two mentioned continue to live up to their own expectations and actively work to make a place for themselves and their peers in a society that has forgotten them.

One of the many ways of combating the lumping syndrome of forcing all people over 65 into one mold is to begin identifying the differences in this highly individuated group of people. With specific developmental tasks spelled out for at least two groups of the elderly—the young-old and the vulnerable old—society can begin to set new norms and to respond to new expectations of these two groups.

The conceptual framework of this chapter is that of Erikson and Havighurst. It is an attempt to examine the developmental tasks of people 60 years of age and older that Havighurist developed and to begin to make them more reflective of the two different groups of elderly in the United States today.

In Chapter 1 the specific story of each group was discussed against a background of the times in which they lived. That same framework of time will be used as a backdrop for the present discussion of the developmental tasks of the young-old (55 to 74) and the vulnerable old (75 and over).

Havighurst's tasks for the older person were as follows:
1. Adjusting to decreasing physical strength and health
2. Adjusting to retirement and reduced income
3. Adjusting to death of spouse
4. Establishing an explicit affiliation with one's age group
5. Meeting social and civic obligations
6. Establishing satisfactory physical living arrangements

In the 1950s and 1960s this was a sufficient delineation of the tasks of the elderly. Almost two decades later, with a qualitatively different cohort in their later fifties to early seventies, those tasks are no longer clear. What follows is an early conceptualization and discussion of the developmental tasks of the two groups of elderly based on the socioeconomic times in which they have lived.

THE YOUNG-OLD

The age group roughly spanning the years from 55 to 74 has come to be known as the young-old, or the self-directed old. In this chapter seven tasks have been identified for each of the two cohorts of elderly persons. Each task will be discussed separately, even though the reader will note that none is discrete and that it is the interdependence of the seven that gives a holistic view of each group.

Preparing for and adjusting to retirement from active involvement in the work arena with its subsequent role change (especially for men). Voluntary early retirement can be an enjoyable change of role to anticipate while one is still young and healthy enough to enjoy the early years of retirement. For older workers and for professionals who have no choice but to face mandatory retirement at 65, this is a traumatic event. Forced retirement at an arbitrarily assigned age, regardless of an individual's functional level, is no longer a good practice in this society.

Because American society has been production oriented, one's major social role is built around one's work. For example, much of the American man's social and cultural norms revolve around occupation. When these norms are abruptly cut off, with nothing but a gold watch for remembrance, workers find themselves anomic in the Durkheimian sense. It should be no surprise that as men move further and further into their rolelessness, they begin to increase the suicide statistics in our society.

Women who have not been active in the paid work arena but whose entire work ethic revolved around homemaking and parenting had to adjust to retirement at an earlier age than did their husbands, probably in their forties or when the last of their children left home.

This retirement from the work arena not only changes one's status in a production-oriented society but also, as will be anticipated later, changes one's status in the economic arena. It also indicates that one needs to reaffirm one's friendships if those have evolved from the work environment, as is true of most workers.

Anticipating and adjusting to lower and fixed income after retirement. For the 55- to 74-year-old age group, adjusting to lower income will not be as traumatic as it has been for their elders. Because they have a higher educational level (50% have completed high school or more) they have had better jobs and better incomes on which to base their retirement income. Regardless of this fact, a fixed income remains so despite recessions and inflation. Although this young-old group has more discretionary dollars at its command for travel, training for a second career, and/or returning to the educational arena, they nonetheless must become aware of the fixed number of dollars. Saving money is imperative lest any long illness or catastrophe face them. For the individual or the married couple formerly able to come and go as they chose, to suddenly have to decide whether they can afford a trip could become a crucial and visible sign of what it means to be retired.

Relatively few resources are available for working with those anticipating their retirement to help them establish a basic financial standard from which they can enjoy their retirement years. Although some companies are taking this as a responsibility, they are in the minority, and it becomes a developmental task of individuals moving into the young-old group to find and establish for themselves satisfactory income adjustments.

Establishing satisfactory physical living arrangements as a result of role changes. In the developmental cycle of the housing industry, individual couples usually begin their lives in small one- or two-bedroom apartments. During the process of childbearing and child rearing, they move to larger homes. When their children begin to leave home, couples tend to retain their homes so that "the children will have some place to come." As couples move into this young-old category, they begin to realize that they neither need the space, nor, if they are anticipating income reduction, can they afford the space. Therefore as they move more toward a couple society again, approximately 20 to 30 years later, the developmental cycle of the housing industry moves toward smaller homes, townhouses, condominiums, or apartments.

If a person has the financial ability to be able to choose where he wants to live and make suitable arrangements, this is not a traumatic move but rather a deliberate choice to reduce the responsibilities of home ownership and increase time to spend on the things that he enjoys. However, if the income has become so fixed that he is forced to continue the developmental cycle of housing, that is, to continue to move to smaller and smaller quarters without much choice, this adds to the trauma of the early aging process.

Adjusting to new relationships with one's adult children and their offspring. For the young-old moving into grandparent roles, it becomes easy to adjust to grandchildren and to do for grandchildren what they either were not able to do or, because of their own child-rearing beliefs, choose not to do with their own children. The grandparent-grandchild relationship, which is the alternate generational relationship, has usually been a highly enjoyable one for the older member of that pair.

What will become difficult now will be a new and changing relationship with adult children. Ordinarily in the socializing cycle, parents have trained and socialized their children to their own values and norms. They have had more wisdom and experience in the live world and have used this to hand down values to their children. However, fast-changing social movements frequently make adult children the socializers of their parents, assisting them to move into new and changing societal norms. This role reversal in the socialization process is difficult for many adults, who find it hard to accept from their adult children the same service that they themselves gave in the original relationship. It is not a fable that alternate generations, grandparents and their grandchildren, have good relationships, and adjacent generations, adults and their adult children, have more stormy relationships. One of the developmental tasks of the young-old group is to learn how to adjust to this new relationship with their adult children without finding it another role loss in their already role-threatened existence.

Learning or continuing to develop leisure-time activities to help in re-alignment of role losses. In this cohort of elderly, many of the young-old have been able to develop leisure-time activities, as couples and as individuals, that will stand them in good stead as they anticipate the move into their retirement years. For many in the upper working class and the middle class, this has become a value for them, and there will be little difficulty in their continuing those activities except insofar as their fixed income becomes a hindrance. However, for others moving into the young-old category who have been work oriented and have had few choices, loss of the work role makes it difficult to fill space and time. It is these people in particular who could adjust and adapt well to the continuing education offered by the local public school systems to help fill their roles. It is also this category of people, as well as those who have developed leisure-time activities, who would do well to involve themselves in such volunteer activities as RSVP, Foster Grandparents, and other programs in which the elderly can be in a position to share their wisdom and experience with younger people.

Anticipating and adjusting to slower physical and intellectual responses in the activities of daily living. Although all people as they age tend to slow in their physical responses, one does not think of one's self as old as one anticipates or begins a retirement phase of life. However, it is true physiologically that the loss of cellular life does slow down the physical responses in the ordinary activities of daily living. One who is used to taking three flights of stairs with no problem or walking several miles a day now finds himself having to slow down and to learn to accept that slowing process without feeling as if he had lost a vital part of himself. Although a majority of the young-old do not experience the slowing in their intellectual activities, enough of them do experience this phenomenon that it should be at least anticipated in terms of possible coping mechanisms. Part of the adjustment to slower activities is eased by the fact that persons are no longer responsible to the pace of the work world and in fact do have more leisure time. Little pressure is put on them to complete tasks except as part of their own behavioral expectations. It is in areas such as this that adult children and others who work with the young-old can help them to adjust without sensing a physiological loss of face with their peers.

Dealing with the death of parents, spouses, and friends. It is in this young-old age of the middle fifties to middle seventies that one begins to deal realistically with the death of parents and spouses. People expect to bury their elders; it has always been so. If it has been a positive relationship that has been lost, the loss will be felt in due degree. If it has been an ambivalent relationship, the grieving is more difficult, since the ambivalence tends to prolong the grief response.

The same is true of spouses. In terms of the actuarial statistics, women may tend to expect that they will bury their husbands. The expectation ordinarily does nothing to ease the pain of loss and the mourning period. In dealing with the death of one's parents, one is faced with a loss that is anticipated and mourned. In dealing with the death of a spouse, one deals with more than the loss of a loved one. A woman also deals with the loss of a role that has been part of her for a number of years. In contemporary American society a single woman, widowed, finds it much more difficult to come back into the social realm. If she is a young widow in her early fifties, she can easily become a threat to friends and peers whose husbands are still alive. If she is one who has enjoyed the company of her husband and their couple-oriented activities, she sustains not only the loss of a spouse but the loss of many friends and role expectations that come in such a couple-oriented society. These losses must also be mourned.

The death of a spouse is neither expected nor usually prepared for. Neither is the death of a friend or peer. This is always difficult. Not only does it involve the loss of a loved person and the loss of role relationships, but it also tends to bring home the fact that one also is mortal. Erikson's sense of "ego chill" is again felt here when one is faced with the reality of one's own mortality.

Summary. These seven, then, are the developmental tasks that have been conceptualized for the younger cohort of elderly, those 55 through 74, known as the young-old. Although they are not discrete developmental tasks, they can be separated and discussed individually, all the while remembering that they are interdependent on one another. If one is to deal with the death of spouses and friends, one must therefore adjust the leisure-time activities one planned and enjoyed with those lost loved ones. If it is necessary to live on lower and fixed incomes, it is also necessary to adjust to affordable leisure-time activities.

However, it is also true that the young-old can be a powerful force in this society for manipulating the various systems that they have helped to create. If the vulnerable old are vulnerable in more ways than their own physiology, it would seem that the young-old who have raised their families and now have some time and discretionary dollars at their disposal are in a unique position to become a powerful political force in developing support and delivery systems that they themselves will need and enjoy when they move into their vulnerable years.

THE VULNERABLE OLD

Chapter 1, which discussed the intergenerational relationships of the vulnerable old and the young-old, made it clear that people 75 years and older are a distinct cohort of elderly. Seventy-two percent of them completed 8 years of formal schooling. They frequently had a language barrier to contend with at their work. Lack of formal education and, for many, an immigrant status combined to force them into unskilled or semiskilled labor. These conditions, in addition to poor (if even existent) pension plans, made it almost impossible for them to accumulate any significant savings for their older years.

These conditions and others discussed at more length in that earlier chapter make this group of elderly much more vulnerable to the ravages of the aging process. Indeed, it becomes difficult to distinguish between the physiological aging process of cell degeneration and decrement and the multiple physical diseases that accompany old age. The majority of the very old are subject to cataracts that diminish visual activity. They sustain hearing losses of certain high tones and decibels. Many suffer from some form of cardiac decompensation and kidney-bladder problems. Diabetes is a common physical problem of the elderly, as is arteriosclerosis.

This may be a depressing view of the very old, but one must keep several things in mind. One is that there *are* the Garson Meyers and the Maggie Kuhns of this world, who are physically and psychologically young for their age. The other fact one must remember is the myth of the lumping syndrome referred to earlier. In this chapter, despite the objection to that syndrome, we do indeed discuss some generalities of a given age group, all the while remembering that although no one person fits all the descriptions, all people reflect some of the details to be discussed.

Before beginning the discussion of the seven developmental tasks identified for this age group, it is important to repeat that no one of these tasks is discrete in and of itself. Some of the more social tasks (as opposed to the more physical ones) will have been faced at earlier stages in the life cycle. Successful completion of them bodes well for the individual: a pattern of successful coping can be relied on for the familiar tasks in this next life stage. However, the opposite can also be true. If one has had difficulty addressing a similar developmental task at an earlier age, one will most likely have difficulty again, especially if one is more vulnerable the next time around.

In a parallel approach, seven developmental tasks have been identified for this cohort of elderly.

Learning to combine new dependency needs with the continuing need for independence. This generation, perhaps more than any other, thrived on its independence. These were the men and women who lived through ''the war to end war,'' the Great Depression, and all the other historical events of the early 1900s. This generation, with generally an eighth-grade education, put their children through high school. They were able to provide a better nutritional level and better preventive health care for their children than they themselves had experienced.

The decades of the seventies and eighties take a physical toll on men and women. As described earlier, multiple diseases and physiological losses are sustained during these years. This generation had little opportunity to make use of the social systems that their adult children helped create. They began benefiting from Social Security, and, once they realized that that system was repaying them their tax money, they could accept it readily and not as charity. However, since Social Security had never been conceived of as a source of total support, even the monthly checks were not enough to pay for rent, food, and medicine.

Not only did the vulnerable old find it difficult to support themselves financially (especially in the inflation of the late 1960s and early 1970s), but more and more found themselves unable to carry out routine activities of daily living without assistance. Old homesteads became dangerous, with narrow, steep stairs, dark hallways, and other structural barriers. When an elderly person suffered a stroke or had to face cataract surgery, kitchens became impossible to work in, and housekeeping became more and more difficult.

Only 7% to 9% of this elderly cohort are institutionalized at any one time, but a large percentage are home-bound because of physical disabilities and architectural barriers in public transportation and buildings. It is this group, perhaps more than the already institutionalized, that need help in identifying areas of their daily lives in which they can retain independent functioning. There is no scientific way yet to slow down the physiological losses in the aging process. There are ways, however, of working with this group to define some areas of independence so that they can accept their necessary dependence with less anguish. Older people expect to lose some of their ability to function independently; they must be helped—and must help themselves—to accept this loss with dignity.

Adapting to living alone in continued independence. The statistics of insurance companies and the U.S. Census Bureau testify to the fact that, for this cohort of elderly, women outnumber men in a ratio of 100 to 64. That single statistic tells much of the need for women to learn—or continue—to live alone in a society oriented toward couples. Even though this developmental task had to be anticipated by the younger cohort of elderly, the actual experience of living alone in a single house or a high-rise apartment presents major difficulties for older women. Frequently they are the targets of crimes and assault. Often they find that the city they helped build has become their enemy and another source of fear.

Within the context of this task, the aging person needs assistance in such things as budgeting and buying food for one person. Frequently, because there is no one to share mealtimes with, the older woman resorts to the widow's diet of toast and tea. Beyond the problem of budgeting for food and other necessities, there is another force at work, especially for widows of the middle class. These women have built part of their identity around familiar neighborhoods and friends. Too often they are placed in a financial position of deciding where to spend their fixed income—on rent or mortgage to stay in a familiar neighborhood or on proper food and necessary medical needs.

In this developmental task especially, there is an area for adult education and anticipatory guidance. Community health nurses oriented to prevention and primary care would be in a unique position to assist the aging person in anticipating some of the problems and in the problem solving of those already identified.

There is a delicate balance to be achieved here in learning to identify the fine line between wanting to continue living in familiar surroundings and being able to remain in the same environment. Frequently it becomes necessary for family members or professionals to intervene when the older woman can no longer continue to live safely by herself.

Learning to accept and adjust to possible institutional living (nursing and/or proprietary homes) . With the loss of health, home, friends, and perhaps kinship support, it becomes necessary to think about the possibility of moving into an institutional setting. When one speaks of institutions, one cannot ignore Goffman's (1961) work on total institutions and their effect on individuals.

If one has been a compliant person during one's adult years, it may be easier to adjust to the routine that another imposes on one. It may not be so difficult to learn to wait, to learn to be satisfied with mass production and loss of some of one's individuality. If, on the other hand, one has prided oneself on having been independent, on having made one's way in a sometimes unfriendly world, then compliance is difficult to learn.

Establishing an affiliation with one's age group. The vulnerable old, although they may be more sensitive to the many systems that society has created, such as Medicare, Medicaid, and nursing homes, still have affiliation needs. Although the disengagement theory has its proponents and although it is true that there are the rocking-chair elderly, there are also individuals in this cohort who are actively involved in senior citizen groups and church societies. Up to 20% of the elders who make use of the federal nutrition centers are in their eighth decade and still functioning independently.

There are some difficulties in addressing this particular task of aging. One takes the risk of establishing relationships with peers who may well have to be buried, and thus one becomes even more vulnerable. Not only does their world shrink in size, but they come face to face all over again with their own mortality. Nonetheless, it is an important task and one of the recurring social tasks that those elderly who wish to maintain their own ego strength must attempt to accomplish.

Learning to adjust to heightened vulnerability to physical and emotional stress. Because this cohort has lived longest in our society, they are a highly individuated group of people. Their repertoire of coping skills is broader and more perfected than that of younger people. Nevertheless, because physiologically their cells are degenerating and their intellectual responses are slower, this group of elderly is more susceptible to levels of stress than are younger cohorts. A person who already suffers from cardiac and vascular problems reacts more quickly and to a greater degree to emotional stresses such as fear or loss of loved ones and to physical trauma such as fractured hips or congestive heart failure.

When an older person can anticipate this possibility, he can begin to rearrange some of the elements of his life-style so as to avoid the sources of such stress. The important thing in such adaptation is to help the older individual develop ego defenses without isolating himself from all normal activity. The old person can overreact in the same way as anyone else. It is important when working with the elderly that their real vulnerability does not assume the posture of immobilizing fear that would incapacitate them even more than is necessitated by the aging process.

Adjusting to loss of physical strength, illness, and the approach of one's death. For the vulnerable old, illness is not a new experience. What is new and, for many, difficult is the slowed response to medical care and the prolonged recuperation periods that follow illness.

When that illness is life threatening, then the older person takes on added worry and concern about his own death. Death is not a new phenomenon to the elderly. They have buried their parents. Some have buried spouses and perhaps children. All have experienced the loss of peers. Anticipating one's own death, however, is qualitatively different. The elderly are a microcosm of the larger population. Some welcome death as the final act of living; others are terrified at the possibility of nonbeing and nothingness. One thing that can be stated rather generally, however, is that for most aging people, the source of fear is not so much that they *will* die but rather how long it will take, where it will happen, and whether they will be alone when they die.

One thing that the elder does—his life review, as Butler (1964) names it—can make a qualitative difference in how he approaches his own death. If that life review process has been positive and the individual has been basically satisfied with the course of his life, it will be easier to face his approaching death. If, on the other hand, an individual has felt cheated by life, passed over, or does not have the satisfaction of having achieved the goals set out at an earlier time, then his death will be more painful to accept. It is in this latter dimension that the older person may need some professional help in facing his own death.

Adjusting to losses of spouse, home, and friends. This particular task may have been faced at an earlier time if one lost a husband, wife, or friends. Such is the case with many of the more social of the developmental tasks. The difference here is the vulnerable position of the individual at this time of life. Any loss becomes more difficult if it is compounded with other stresses.

Although it is not included as a developmental task per se, it seems necessary at this point to speak of the possibility of adjusting to the loss of one's children. When one reaches the eighth and ninth decades, there is a greater probability that one may well have to face the death of a child. Although the developmental clock would ordinarily predict that children bury their elders, the reverse is too often true. Again it becomes more difficult when one is generally more vulnerable in other areas as well.

The loss of one's home is also hard for this cohort to accept. This generation of home owners have probably been more stable than their succeeding generations. The current middle-years cohort (35 to 55) are predicted to relocate on the average of seven times, but the vulnerable old have been much more stable in their homes.

Especially for women in this age group, the home and its homemaker role have been a major part of their ego identity. To face the loss of a home (be it a one-family dwelling or an apartment) is to face the loss of one of the last independent components in one's role set. It is more than relocation that one must anticipate; it is also a final breaking up of roles, norms, expectations, and statuses in an individual already stressed to the extreme.

FURTHER STUDY NEEDED

Because the young-old and the vulnerable old are qualitatively different it seemed logical to think about some of the developmental tasks they would face. Havighurst first began identifying in broad strokes some of the tasks an older generation might face. His was the original work from which this chapter has sprung. The ideas and discussion here are the first articulation of what may become a basis for further research on the two cohorts of older people in our society.

Earlier in this chapter, concern was expressed about the lumping syndrome and the continued stereotyping of the elderly. Yet it can be argued that this chapter has done the same thing, although in smaller age groups. That is precisely why this chapter can be only the *beginning* of research on the concept of developmental tasks in these two cohorts.

The tasks discussed here are of necessity generic. I have not discussed ethnic differences, various socioeconomic strata in the society, or the issue of individuals who for various reasons have to face some of their developmental tasks out of time. For instance, I have discussed the developmental task of learning to combine new dependency needs with a need for continuing independence. That task demands completely different responses from a 78-year-old man than from a 43-year-old man who has suffered major cardiac damage. The whole concept of being on time or out of time is only one of a number of interactive effects that must be addressed in the ongoing research of developmental tasks in the life cycle.

It is my desire that indeed this chapter be only the beginning of the study of developmental tasks in the elderly.

REFERENCES

Butler, R. The life review: an interpretation of reminiscence in the aged. In Kastenbaum, R. (Ed.).
   New thoughts on old age. New York: Springer Publishing Co., Inc., 1964.
Durkheim, Emil. *Suicide*. Glencoe, Ill.: The Free Press, 1951.
Erikson, Erik. *Childhood and society* (2nd ed.). New York: W. W. Norton & Co., Inc., 1950.
Goffman, Erving. *Asylums*. New York: Doubleday & Co., Inc., 1961.
Havighurst, Robert. *Developmental tasks and education*. New York: David McKay Co., Inc., 1973.

DEVELOPMENTAL PERSPECTIVES

Bernice L. Neugarten, Ph.D.*

As a developmental psychologist interested in creating a broadly-based developmental behavioral science, I should like to introduce my comments by saying that we need a psychology of the life-cycle—a psychology that will view the life-cycle as an appropriate unit for study, one that will encompass child development, adolescent development, adult development, aging, and the relationships between them. A psychology of the life-cycle would help to produce, in turn, a psychiatry of the life-cycle, one in which the relations between mental illness and mental health, pathology and non-pathology, would be examined always in light of development principles and age-related personality processes. Both the psychology and the psychiatry of the life-cycle are concerned with questions of continuities and discontinuities in the life history, or, in other words, with problems of stability and change in personality. Closely related is the problem of delineating the social and psychologic issues that arise at consecutive age periods in the life-cycle and differentiating those that are age-specific from those that are not. A second set of problems is concerned with individual differences between persons as they go fron infancy to old age.

In considering developmental perspectives of the aging process, I want briefly to comment upon and to illustrate these problems. In each instance, I shall be drawing upon various sets of empirical studies carried on by myself and my colleagues in the Committee on Human Development at the University of Chicago, studies of large samples of middle-aged and older men and women, all of them living in the metropolitan areas of Kansas City or Chicago, and all of them living what we like to call ''normal'' lives.

Reproduced from Psychiatric Research Reports of the American Psychiatric Association, February, 1968, **23,**42-48.
*Professor of Human Development, University of Chicago, Chicago, Illinois.

CHANGE IN PERSONALITY IN MIDDLE AND OLD AGE

While in many ways personality seems to remain relatively stable in middle and old age, in other ways measurable changes do occur. Because this field has as yet attracted only a few investigators, the picture is at best incomplete. Let me illustrate, however, from a series of studies based on various interview data and projective test data gathered from representative groups aged forty to eighty.

Significant and consistent age differences were found in both working-class and middle-class people in the perception of the self *vis-à-vis* the external environment and in their coping with impulse life. Forty-year-olds, for example, seem to see the environment as one that rewards boldness and risk-taking and to see themselves as possessing energy congruent with the opportunities perceived in the outer world. Sixty-year-olds, on the other hand, seem to perceive the world as complex and dangerous, no longer to be reformed in line with one's wishes, and the individual as conforming and less accommodating to outer-world demands.

Important differences exist between men and women as they age. Men seem to become more receptive to affiliative and nurturant promptings, women more responsive to and less guilty about aggressive and egocentric impulses. Men appear to cope with the environment in increasingly abstract and cognitive terms, women in increasing affective and expressive terms. In both sexes older people move toward more egocentric, self-preoccupied positions and attend increasingly to control and satisfaction of personal needs.

With increasing old age, ego functions are turned inward, as it were. There is a change from active to passive modes of mastering the environment, and there is also a movement of energy away from an outer-world to an inner-world orientation, a change we called an increased "interiority" of personality.*

Whether or not this increased interiority has inherent as well as reactive qualities cannot yet be established—that is, whether there are time-related changes in personality that are reflections of biologic changes in the organism and are relatively independent of the environment, or whether the changes we see are in reaction to or in response to (or in anticipation of) changes in the social environment. It may be that in advanced old age biologically based factors become the pace-makers of personality changes; but this question awaits further disentangling of the effects of illness from the effects of aging *per se,* effects that presently are confounded in most older persons who are the subjects of psychologic research.

Some of our colleagues at Chicago broadened the interpretation of these findings, looked at some of our other findings regarding social participation patterns, and then set forth the "disengagement theory" (Cumming and Henry, 1961). That theory says, in essence, that people as they age withdraw from social

---

*These findings have been described at greater length in Neugarten and associates (1964).

and psychologic involvements in the environment at the same time that society withdraws its support from the aged person. In other words, there is a mutual process by which the individual shows a withdrawal phenomenon at the same time that, for various reasons, such as death of friends, death of spouse, or retirement, he suffers a series of social losses outside his control.

For the first part of the life span it appears that persons develop abilities, skills, and sets of psychologic mechanisms for dealing with the world, and their attention is given generally to managing the self and to practicing the techniques for dealing with an ever-widening world of experience. In middle age there is a reorganization and a re-evaluation of the self, a change in the quality of social interaction, and the beginning of a kind of interiority that involves a preoccupation with the inner life and new methods of dealing with impulse life. The major change-over probably begins in middle age, not in old age, although the processes are more characteristic of the old person. Thus, not all the withdrawal seen in very aged persons can be attributed to events that are happening in the family or in the work situation or in the kinds of losses that people experience as they age. Some of the withdrawal is probably "natural" in the sense that it is characteristic of most people as they move through the years from fifty to eighty.

The disengagement theory was, in part, a restatement of the everyday observation that persons as they grow old lose a great many of their social and psychologic ties to the environment. It was new in stating that aging is probably accompanied by some kinds of inner processes that make the loosening of social ties a relatively natural process.

The disengagement theory has been modified in the past few years, not only by its original authors, but by others of us who have continued to analyze the data on which it was based.* The modification has to do, not with those parts of the theory dealing with the loosening of social ties or psychologic withdrawal, but with those dealing with the postulated relationship between disengagement and well-being. It is now apparent on the whole, and contrary to the first statement of the disengagement theory, that persons who remain relatively active in the various social roles of family member, citizen, club member, friend, and so on, are the persons who report themselves most content with their lives. Thus, while it is likely that certain types of social loss and certain types of psychologic withdrawal are characteristic of most people as they grow old, it is simultaneously true that persons in whom these processes are most marked are not necessarily the happiest—as might have been predicted from a knowledge of the social values that characterize the American society.

In any case, the personality changes that I have mentioned are useful in the present context to illustrate that personality changes occur in the last half as well

---

*The disengagement theory was first set forth by Cumming and Henry (1961). It has since been modified in such papers as Cumming (1963), Henry (1963), Havighurst, Neugarten, and Tobin (1964), and Neugarten (1965).

as in the first half of the life cycle and to illustrate the problems of charting continuities and discontinuities from the point of view of a developmental perspective of the aging process.

INDIVIDUAL DIFFERENCES

The developmental psychologist is interested in discovering the similarities among people as they grow up and grow old; but he is interested also in discovering the differences. I have just illustrated a few of the personality changes that are characteristic of persons as they move from middle into old age; the same series of studies are useful to illustrate the great differences that exist.

. There are many stereotypes in our society about old people growing more and more alike, but in our community samples we have been impressed with the way people grow more unlike. Indeed, it is probably an accurate view that differentiation continues throughout the lifetime and grows greater rather than less, until perhaps very advanced old age—perhaps at the very end of life—when biologic impairments may become so large that they limit and therefore narrow the variety of patterns of adaptation.

As researchers we tried to develop measures that would distinguish various phenomena: social role activity, personality pattern, and happiness (or life satisfaction).

One can, for instance, interview people at length and find out how much of their time is given to one after another social role—that is, how much time does the person spend in his role as spouse, or homemaker, or parent, or worker, or church member, or citizen, or club member, and so on—and one can say that one person is much higher in role performance than another person. At the same time, the researcher can develop a set of psychologic measures of how people structure their environments, what their inner feelings are, their self-concepts, and so on, and from these measures work out a system of personality types. Third, the researcher can measure how content or satisfied people are with their lives. If these are regarded as three somewhat independent measures, then one can study the relationships between these measures and, by so doing, describe the patterns of aging to be found in a community sample. In somewhat different words, we asked, what are the varieties of socio-psychologic patterns to be found? What situations produce greater satisfaction with life, given a certain kind of personality to start with?

Every individual is different from every other, of course, but we grouped individuals on the basis of similarities and differences on the three measures just mentioned. Let me describe the patterns of aging that emerged in persons who were aged seventy to seventy-nine. (The nature and variety of the patterns are somewhat different for younger and for older persons.)

The majority of our seventy-year-olds remained what we called *integrated* personalities: well-functioning persons with complex inner lives and intact cognitive abilities and competent egos. These persons were accepting of impulse life, over which they maintained a comfortable degree of control; they were flexible, open to new stimuli, mellow, mature. All these individuals, it happens, were rated high in life satisfaction. At the same time, they differed with regard to role activity: One group fell into a pattern we call the "reorganizers," who are the competent people engaged in a wide variety of activities. They are the optimum agers in some respects—at least in the American culture, where there is a high value placed on "staying young, staying active, and refusing to grow old." These are persons who substitute new activities for lost ones; who, when they retire from work, give time to community affairs or to church or to other associations. They reorganize their patterns of activity. A second pattern among the integrated personalities we call the "focused." These are integrated personalities with high life satisfaction, who show only medium levels of activity. They have become selective in their activities, and they devote energy to one or two role areas. One such person, for instance, was a retired man who was now preoccupied with the roles of homemaker, parent, and husband. He had withdrawn from work and from club memberships and welcomed the opportunity to live a happy life with his family, seeing his children and grandchildren, gardening, and helping his wife with homemaking, which he had never done before. The third pattern we call the "disengaged." These are also integrated personalities, with high life satisfaction but low activity; persons who have voluntarily moved away from role commitments, not in response to external losses or physical deficits, but out of preference. These are self-directed persons, not shallow, with an interest in the world, but an interest that is not imbedded in a network of social interactions. They have high feelings of self-regard, just as do the first two groups mentioned, but they have chosen what might be called a "rocking chair" approach to old age—a calm, withdrawn, but contented pattern.

A second category includes the men and women whose personality type we call *armored* or *defended*. These are the striving, ambitious, achievement-oriented personalities, with high defenses against anxiety and the need to maintain tight controls over impulse life. This personality group provides two patterns of aging: one we call the "holding-on" pattern. This is the group to whom aging constitutes a threat, and who respond by holding on, as long as possible, to the patterns of their middle age. They are quite successful in their attempts, and thus maintain high life satisfaction with medium or high activity levels. These are persons who say, "I'll work until I drop," or "So long as you keep busy, you will get along all right." The other pattern we call the "constricted." These are persons busily defending themselves against aging, preoccupied with losses and deficits, dealing with these threats by constricting their social interactions and their energies and by closing themselves off from experience. They seem to structure their worlds to keep off what they regard as imminent collapse; and while this constriction results in low role activity, it works fairly well, given their personality pattern, to keep them high or medium in life satisfaction.

The third group of personalities is the *passive-dependent* type, among whom there are two patterns of aging. The "succorance-seeking" are those who have strong dependency needs and who seek responsiveness from others. These persons maintain medium levels of activity and medium levels of life satisfaction, and seem to maintain themselves fairly well so long as they have at least one or two other persons whom they can lean on and who meet their emotional needs. The "apathetic" pattern represents those persons in whom passivity is a striking feature of personality and who exhibit low role activity and medium or low life satisfaction. These are also "rocking chair" people, but with very different personality structures from those we have called the "disengaged." This apathetic pattern seems to occur in persons in whom aging probably has reinforced long-standing patterns of passivity and apathy. Here, for instance, was a man who, in the interviews, was content to let his wife do his talking for him, and a woman whose activities were limited entirely to maintaining her physical needs.

Finally, there is a group of *unintegrated* personalities who show a disorganized pattern of aging. These persons have gross defects in psychologic function, loss of control over emotions, and deterioration in thought processes. They maintain themselves in the community, but are low both in role activity and in life satisfaction.

The eight patterns do not exhaust all the varieties to be found in our group of seventy-year-olds, but given even this diversity, it is variation rather than similarity that is impressive. There is an implication, also, that the basic pattern of aging might be predicted for a given individual, given sufficient information about his personality and his general pattern of adaptation at an earlier age—say, at age fifty. (Given, also, of course, no overwhelming biologic accidents occurring to the subject.) It is, once again, the questions of continuity and discontinuity and of the range of individual differences that develop over time that preoccupy the developmental psychologist. To him, old age is not a separate and unique stage of life; to him the problems of the aged and the study of aging are to be seen within the complex of biologic, socio-cultural, and personal variation that provides the context for studying all stages of life.

REFERENCES

Cumming, E. 1963. Further thoughts on the theory of disengagement. Int. Soc. Sci. J. **15:**337-393.

Cumming, E. and Henry, W. E. 1961. Growing old. New York: Basic Books.

Havighurst, R. J., Neugarten, B. L., and Tobin, S. S. 1964. Disengagement, personality and life satisfaction in the later years. In P. F. Hansen (Ed.), Age with A Future. Copenhagen: Munksgaard, pp. 419-425.

Henry, W. E. 1963. The theory of intrinsic disengagement. Paper read at the International Research Seminar on Social and Psychological Aspects of Aging, Markaryd, Sweden, August, 1963.

Neugarten, B. L. 1965. Personality and patterns of aging. J. of Psychology of the University of Nijemegen (Gawein) **13:**249-256.

Neugarten, B. L., and associates. 1964. Personality in Middle and Late Life. New York: Atherton.

AGE WITH A FUTURE

Nathan W. Shock, Ph.D.*

"Father Time is not always a hard parent, and, though he tarries for none of his children, often lays his hand lightly on those who have used him well"—Charles Dickens in "Barnaby Rudge."

The title of this paper is intentionally ambiguous. From it none of you can know whether I plan to write about babies or senescents, since both age. Actually, what I propose to discuss is the total life-span but with special emphasis on the later years.

As indicated, aging is a general universal process which takes place over the entire life-span. The life-span of the human may be roughly divided into three major divisions. During the first 20 years, or even 25 years, of existence, the individual is maturing or learning, but he is also aging. The next 40 years constitute the normal working life. The third period, which may be characterized as the post-retirement period, extends now, for the most part, simply by administrative fiat, from age 65 onward. On the average, this amounts to an additional ten years of life for men and about 17 years for women. These figures represent the best estimates for continued life in individuals who have reached the age of 65. In this paper I would like to explore the potentialities of the post-retirement period and to consider the prospects for improving and extending this period of life.

It must be recognized that the age of retirement is very arbitrary and one which has been fixed in our society as age 65. When the age of 65 was chosen, it was expected that most individuals would spend only about five years in retire-

Reproduced from *The Gerontologist*, Autumn, 1968, **8**,147-152.
*Gerontology Research Center, National Institute of Child Health and Human Development, National Institutes of Health, PHS, U.S. Department of Health, Education and Welfare, Bethesda, and the Baltimore City Hospitals, Baltimore, Maryland.

ment. Now, however, it is apparent that most of us will spend considerably more than five years in retirement. Retirement in the future will be even longer since it will begin earlier and last longer. Current trends in technology lead to the prediction that within the foreseeable future the age of retirement for many workers will be lowered to 55.

It is also probable that with advances in medical science there will be a further extension of life-span of as much as five to ten years. Thus, it is increasingly clear that the post-retirement period will encompass a greater proportion of the life-span than it now does and may well represent the period of life when people can reach their ultimate goals of personal achievement and satisfaction. The burning question is, "What do we propose to do with these added years?"

What are the factors that set a limit on longevity? It is well known that different animals differ widely in their life-span; thus the house fly lives about 90 days, the rat two to three years, the dog 12 to 15, the horse 15 to 20, and man 90 to 100. It is, therefore, clear that the genetic makeup includes some program for aging. Differences in this program, or rate of aging, are present even between individuals within a given species. For example, it has been possible to produce two separate strains of mice, one of which lives only about 12 months whereas the other lives 24 months. Even in man it has been shown that individuals with long lived ancestors live on the average four or five years longer than individuals whose parents and grandparents died at an early age. However, basic biologic research has been able to show that whatever this basic genetic pattern of aging is, it can be altered by environmental factors.

In order to conduct experiments of this kind, the investigator must turn to some species other than man. In our laboratory, Dr. Barrows and his associates have studied the effect of changes in temperature and in nutrition on the life-span of the rotifer. The rotifer is a small aquatic animal about the size of a pin-head. It is an ideal animal for these experiments because many individuals can be hatched from eggs laid by the same mother. Since no father is required for this animal, each of the individuals derived from the same mother will have exactly the same genetic program. Since the animal is cold blooded it is also possible to alter its body temperature simply by altering the temperature of the water in which it lives.

Now under normal circumstances this animal has a life-span of approximately 34 days, distributed as follows: four days of development after hatching, 11 to 15 days of active egg laying, and approximately 18 days of "retirement." When the temperature of the animal is raised slightly, that is, from 25° to 35° C. its life-span drops to about 18 days but all of the loss in total life-span comes out of the "retirement" period.

In contrast, life-span can be increased from the normal 34 days to as much as 55 days simply by reducing the food supply available to the animal. However, this alteration in environment does not affect the "retirement" period of life which remains at 18 days. Instead, starvation lengthens life-span by increasing the period of egg-laying from 11 to 29 days, although the total number of eggs laid is the same as in well fed rotifers—it simply takes longer to produce them. The same genetic program for the rotifer can be lengthened or shortened by changes in environmental conditions.

These experimental conditions cannot be applied to the human but they are of extreme importance in showing that the genetic pattern of aging can be influenced by environmental factors. As the biologist generates more basic knowledge about the mechanisms of aging, applications which will benefit people will eventually evolve.

The second most important factor that influences the life-span of the human is disease, of which heart disease, high blood pressure, cancer, and respiratory diseases such as pneumonia are the primary culprits. Arthritis is another common disease; however, it does not kill but produces disability, especially among the elderly.

A third factor which limits longevity is obesity. This is a persistent remedial problem especially among the middle aged.

A fourth factor which limits longevity is the gradual change in organs and tissues which results in a reduction of reserve capacity. These changes do not proceed uniformly in all organ systems and may or may not be the inevitable consequences of aging. It is in this area that a great deal of research needs to be done. We do know that many of these changes can be compensated for by prosthetic devices such as glasses, hearing aids, dentures, etc., and that others can be retarded in their progression by systematic exercise and activities. Others can be lived with simply by avoiding the strain of excesses. A brief future for the aged will stem from (a) contributions of research, (b) the application of medical advances which in turn will be the outgrowth of basic scientific research, (c) the effects of social changes, and (d) the enlightened efforts of the individual.

CONTRIBUTION OF RESEARCH

The problems of aging have been systematically studied only in the past few years. There is a rising interest in studies on the causes of aging at the biological and cellular level but much remains to be done. Few investigators even now are directly concerned with these fundamental problems. In recognition of the need for more investigators in the field of aging, the National Institutes of Health are now supporting some 22 training programs in various aspects of gerontology which have been established in different universities in the United States. Many of these programs are just getting under way and it will be three to five years before a significant number of trained investigators becomes available. However, it is a hopeful sign and a move in the right direction.

Recently a panel of experts of the Rand Corporation has estimated anticipated breakthroughs in various aspects of technology and science. One of their predictions is that by the year 2025 the chemical control of aging will be possible. According to their estimates, artificial organs made of plastic and electronic components will be available by 1990. Biochemicals to stimulate growth of new organs and limbs are predicted by 2020. All of these predictions may sound like science fiction, who could have predicted 50 years ago that satellites could be put into orbit and a ''soft'' landing could be made on a pre-selected spot on the moon?

A great deal of research is now being directed toward the underlying causes of many diseases such as heart disease, hardening of the arteries, high blood pressure, cancer, etc. From such research many new drugs for the treatment of high blood pressure and heart disease have been developed. New enzymes have been found which will dissolve blood clots, and intensive efforts are being made to adapt them for use in the human.

One of the important problems for the future is the training of physicians in the special problems of older people. Whether this will be called training in geriatrics or internal medicine is of little consequence. The important issue is that departments of medicine in all medical schools need to develop an awareness among young physicians of the physiological characteristics of older people which are important in treating their ailments and diseases.

Perhaps the most spectacular medical advances have occurred in surgery. Artificial tubing can now be substituted for blood vessels which have become blocked. By restoring the blood supply with such artificial blood vessels, many arms and legs which previously had to be amputated can now be saved. Restoring an adequate blood supply to the head with an artificial blood vessel has produced truly remarkable recovery from the effects of stroke in some patients. This technique will undoubtedly be further explored and extended.

I cannot refrain from pointing out that these benefits to patients stemmed from the results of basic research in organic chemistry which made possible the production of plastic and nylon tubes which can be transplanted into the body and do not cause blood to clot. These artificial materials were developed by organic chemists who were originally interested in the chemistry of polymer formation rather than the production of a piece of tubing which could be used inside the body to transport blood.

The development of new synthetic materials has also made possible the construction of artificial valves which can now be transplanted into the human heart to replace leaky ones. Engineering developments such as miniature circuits and batteries have permitted the development of an artificial device known as a ''pacemaker'' which maintains the heart beat at a regular rate in a patient whose heart misses beats.

A dramatic goal of modern surgery is the transplantation of tissues and organs from one human being to another and ultimately perhaps from animals to man. Transplantation of the kidney, liver, lung, heart, and skin as well as the hormone secreting glands represent ultimate goals. The obstacles that stood in the way of achieving this ambition were surgical, immunological, logistic, and moral. Transplantation of skin from one part of the body to another part in the same person has been possible for a long time, largely because the rejection of the skin by immunological reactions is not a major problem. The grafted skin is recognized by the body as part of itself.

Kidney grafts are also feasible where the donor is a close blood relative of the recipient. Rejection reactions are much less severe toward tissues from close relatives who are apt to be more similar genetically than are people in general. Some of these kidney grafts have remained viable for as long as two to three years. As evidenced by the recent transplantations of human hearts at least the surgical aspects of the problem have been resolved. It is still a moot question as to whether the immunological problems have as yet been solved. The problem is to suppress the immunological responses of the body which reject the grafted organ as a foreign body. Although there are now drugs and methods to accomplish this goal, they are not specific so that the patient loses his ability to fight off any infection. Within the next few years drugs or techniques will probably be developed which will suppress immunologic reaction to heart or kidney tissue but leave intact the ability of the body to produce antibodies against infections.

The logistic problem is one of finding and matching an appropriate donor for each recipient, since we are still a long way from being able to maintain organ banks, although some progress is being made.

At the present time, kidney transplantations are made from living relatives to the patient. This system is possible, since each of us has two kidneys and we can get along pretty well with only one. However, for single organs like the heart, transplants must be made within a short time of the death of the donor. Securing appropriate donors will remain a persistent problem even after all the technical problems are solved.

In my opinion the best escape from the problem of securing donor hearts lies in the development of an artificial pump which can replace the human heart. In the United States a great deal of emphasis is being given to the development of such a device. Engineers, biologists, and physicians are working collaboratively in order to solve the many problems involved. There is, however, no reason a solution, at least for an artificial heart, should not be forthcoming within the foreseeable future.

With the transplantation of other organs the current research approach is to develop techniques whereby organs such as kidney or liver of lower animals can be transplanted to the human. The biological and physiological problems involved in the production of an artificial kidney are much more difficult than for the artificial heart so that the solution is undoubtedly much farther in the future.

The moral problems involved in the transplantation of organs from one human to another are only now becoming apparent. How far are we justified in lowering a donor's expectation of life to prolong the recipient's? What kinds of controls would be required to prevent exploitation of some individuals to provide a source of organs appropriate for transplantation? With the development of artificial organs such as artificial hearts, what limit should be set upon the prolongation of life by these devices? How long should a vegetable existence be extended by artificial means? These are all questions which must be faced by all of us and not just by physicians. Fortunately, we will not be faced with this problem on a mass basis suddenly. It will develop slowly and gradually.

Impending social changes will also play a role in extending the post-retirement period and improving its quality. As previously pointed out, technological advances will undoubtedly tend to lower the age of compulsory retirement. At the same time we can expect a reduction in the length of the work week. This means that during the period of working life more leisure time will become available. With the development of nonworking outside activities, the transition from work to retirement will become less abrupt and, therefore, less traumatic.

With more time available, the worker can engage in many pursuits which can be expanded when he reaches retirement. The middle-aged worker will have more time for community, recreational, and cultural activities than he does at present. He can prepare himself for a second career. A second career does not imply paid employment. A second career may be an activity that is significant and satisfying to the individual. It may range from participation in volunteer community services to fishing, bird watching, or stamp collecting. Its essential characteristic is satisfaction to the individual.

The increasing number of elderly people and lengthening of the post-retirement period demand a redefinition of the role of the elderly. Elderly people must not be regarded simply as a group for whom special services must be provided. Instead they must be regarded as participants in community life. The Age and Opportunity Bureau and other similar organizations must lead the way in demonstrating opportunities for significant roles for the aged within the community.

Senior Centers play an important role in developing social contacts. They have also served as a focal point for cultural and recreational activities. Since only about 5% of the retired population now participate in Senior Center activities, it is apparent that many more are needed and new methods are needed to attract more participants. One approach is to expand programs to channel the efforts of elderly people into useful and significant community activities. This will require not only changes in social customs but also changes in the attitudes of older people. Older individuals, especially men, must be convinced that a pay check is not the only criterion of significant work and efforts. Traditionally, voluntary work within the community is regarded as quite respectable for women but not necessarily for men. This attitude is one which must be overcome if we are to provide meaningful activities for older people.

Ten years ago it was generally assumed that retirement was looked upon as a threat by many people. It was only after research studies directed by Dr. Havighurst and his colleagues in Kansas City that it became apparent that this desire for continued employment was primarily a reflection of the attitudes of professional people and that many older workers looked forward to and actually enjoyed retirement. Hence, the assumption that *all* older people wish to continue to work is wrong. At present over half of the individuals who apply for Social Security benefits in the United States are less than 65 years of age. This is true in spite of the fact that those who retire at age 62 get only 80% of the monthly benefits they would get if they waited until they were 65. It is suggested that one of the reasons so many people are choosing to retire at 62 is that employment opportunities for them have fallen off sharply, in an age stressing automation. Nevertheless, it is apparent that retirement is becoming an acceptable way of life for an increasing proportion of the population.

Social changes will also improve pension benefits. These improvements will accrue not only from increases in benefits such as those enacted by the last Congress of the United States but also from maturation of the retirement program itself. More people will have accumulated increased credits by virtue of longer participation in the program and, therefore, will receive higher retirement incomes.

There should also be marked reduction in the anxiety of aging people with respect to costs for hospitalization and medical care. The enactment of the Medicare program in the United States has provided a firm basis for these services for all people over the age of 65. This program should also improve the health of older people by making available medical services for the treatment of diseases and impairments before they become acute critical problems. It is, therefore, apparent that resources will be available for improving the health status of the elderly. The effectiveness of such programs will depend heavily upon providing physicians, hospitals, and nursing homes as recommended by Dr. Sherman and his committee in a recent report.

Other social programs which will improve the quality of living for elderly people include the development of housing facilities. For the more affluent elderly people, private housing projects and apartment blocks are springing up in many areas of the United States. For those with limited incomes, the requirement established in some states, such as New York, that a certain percentage of the units in public housing projects be allocated to the use of elderly people is a step in the right direction. Federal assistance to non-profit organizations prepared to sponsor construction of new apartments for the elderly has served to stimulate construction of additional units. This trend will continue over the coming years so that improved housing will become more generally available.

There will also be an extension and improvement in services for older people. Homemaker services, day centers, meals on wheels, counseling services, and activity centers will be provided in more and more places through the activities of various agencies. One area which needs extensive exploration is the extent to which elderly people themselves can, through their volunteer activities, provide such services. All of these social changes will contribute greatly to the quality of living in the post-retirement years.

Although research and advances in medical sciences and cultural changes will contribute a great deal to the opportunities of older people for the significant use of their post-retirement years, there are a good many things that the individual himself must do to get the most out of his retirement years. The aging individual must recognize the opportunities that lie before him. First and foremost is the opportunity to be one's self. Freed from economic and social demands of rearing a family, the individual now has the opportunity to choose his own activities and to set his own time schedules. The important point is that, whereas during working life many of his goals have been set by the demands of employment, family, and the need for progressive achievement, the individual now must set his own goals. His goals must be both immediate and long term. It seems to me that perhaps one of the best estimates of the age of an individual would be to inquire about his future plans. As long as the individual has long-term plans he is not really old. He is only old when he has lost all incentive to make plans for his future.

Individuals can also increase their probability of enjoying a long and healthy life by paying closer attention to the quantity and quality of their diet. On the quantitative side, food intake should be adjusted to avoid the accumulation of fat. Insurance statistics show clearly that obesity is associated with an increase in cardiovascular disease and a reduction in life-span.

In a recent study conducted by Dr. Solomon 107 obese men (aged 25-35) who were otherwise normal had decreased biological function tests similar to those of chronologically older men. The greater the obesity, the greater was the impairment. Fifty per cent overweight in a 25-year-old man was associated with functions of heart, lung and kidney and exercise performance found in normal men aged 50. Fifty-two of the originally obese patients reduced to and maintained their ideal weights for one year. At this time, their test results corresponded to those of their chronological age group (25 years). The other 55 patients who remained obese showed no change in their biological tests when repeated a year later.

Although a program of weight reduction will have some beneficial effect, the scars of obesity will remain in the form of sagging skin where the fat came off. This is because one of the basic characteristics of aging is a gradual loss in the elasticity not only of skin but also of blood vessels and other tissues. The old skin is unable to snap back and adjust itself to the new volume once it has been stretched out of shape by the accumulation of fat. Although biologists are engaged in research which may ultimately lead to the development of drugs which can restore the elastic properties to tissues, this goal may be a long way off. It is much better to *keep* slim than to *get* slim.

Since hardening of the arteries is a disease which afflicts a large proportion of elderly people to various degrees and is responsible for heart attacks and strokes, everyone is interested in any method which will prevent the disease or slow it down.

It is now commonly believed that a reduction in fat intake or a shift from the consumption of animal (saturated) fat to vegetable oils (unsaturated) fats will do this. The thesis is that (1) coronary artery disease is associated with high levels of cholesterol and fats in the blood, (2) the level of fats in the blood can be lowered by reducing fat intake and by substituting vegetable oils for animal fat, and (3) lowering the levels of fat and cholesterol in the blood will slow down the rate of development of arteriosclerosis.

The difficulty is that there are still some uncertainties with regard to each of these assumptions that must be resolved by further research. In 1961 the Central Committee for Medical and Community programs of the American Heart Association issued a report on the best scientific information available. It states "reduction or control of fat consumption under medical supervision with reasonable substitution of poly-unsaturated fats is recommended as a possible means in preventing atherosclerosis and decreasing the risk of heart attacks and strokes . . . more complete information must be obtained before final conclusions can be reached." In 1968 the situation remains essentially the same, although large scale studies are now in progress to test the effects of reduction of fat in the diet on the incidence of arteriosclerosis in well controlled populations.

The studies are extremely difficult to carry out and require a long time before definitive results can be obtained. In the meantime we are again faced with basing action on statistical probabilities. At the present time, a reasonable reduction in the intake of fat, especially animal fat, is probably of benefit to (1) the overweight, (2) those who have already had a heart attack or stroke, and (3) those whose personal family histories suggest that they might be particularly susceptible to arteriosclerosis. There is certainly no final proof as yet that dietary changes can prevent heart attacks or strokes in specific individuals.

The qualitative aspects of diet are also important in health maintenance. Although there is no evidence that normal aging people require special supplements of vitamins, proteins, calcium, and other specific nutrients, diets may get out of balance when only a few restricted foods are eaten. Many elderly people are prone to restrict their diet to a few foods that are easily prepared and relatively cheap. Such a program can easily generate a variety of nutritional deficiencies. Special health foods represent primarily an added expense. All foods are basically healthy and the best protection against nutritional deficiencies is to consume a wide variety of foods under the same rules of nutrition that have been developed for the middle aged.

Another environmental factor which influences health and is under the direct control of the individual is cigarette smoking. There is no question that cigarette smoking is associated with an increase in the incidence of lung cancer and cardiovascular disease. It is, of course, true that some individuals who are heavy cigarette smokers never develop these diseases. Neither can it be shown that non-smokers never develop them. It is still a question of probability and the individual must decide for himself the extent to which he wishes to gamble with his own life-span.

Armed with knowledge gained from research about the general changes which occur with aging, individuals can take many active steps to minimize or even to avoid their effects. For example, sensory impairments that occur with advancing age can in many instances be corrected. The impairment in accommodation in vision can readily be corrected by proper fitting of bifocal lenses. Other visual impairments that make reading difficult can be compensated for simply by increasing the level of illumination. A 100-watt bulb to replace the 60-watt bulb can often make a world of difference. The decrease in night vision and increased susceptibility to glare may require the elimination of automobile driving at night but is not an unsurmountable obstacle. Hearing loss which is usually associated with aging can usually be compensated for by hearing aids. Dentures will replace missing teeth, and so on.

Lapses in immediate memory are both frustrating and irritating. It cannot be denied that they occur with increasing frequency as we get older. However, on a quantitative basis, the degree of memory loss with normal aging is not impressive. Although it has recently been reported that extracts of DNA and of chemicals which can be taken in the form of a pill result in substantial improvement of memory in elderly people, these reports must still be substantiated by extensive experimental work. I have no doubt that ultimately such aids will be developed. However, in the meantime we must rely on the usual devices such as writing things down or over-learning them by repetition. The fact has been shown that when older people are permitted to learn new material at their own pace, there is little difference between the learning ability of elderly Ss and young adults. Other aids to learning include actual speaking of the material or seeing and hearing it simultaneously.

In view of the known reduction in reserve capacity, it is important that aging people should reduce their exposure to unusual stresses. They should, however, maintain a program of planned activities that are both satisfying and meaningful. Oftentimes what passes as aging is nothing more than an atrophy of disuse. This is especially true within the sphere of mental activities. A good dictum would be to learn something new every day even if it comes under the heading of useless information. We might well adapt the Boy Scout dictum of ''a good deed every day'' to ''a new deed every day'' for the maintenance of health and vigor in the later years.

In summary I want to emphasize the expanding opportunities for the elderly. The combination of progress in basic research, medical skills, industrial technology, and social organization will increase the post-retirement period. This can represent the period of maximum fulfillment for the individual who seizes the opportunities and makes the most of them.

THE FORESHORTENED LIFE PERSPECTIVE

Robert Kastenbaum, Ph.D.*

The elderly person is marked in more ways than one. His face, hands, and all those body parts which are significant in social communication have become unmistakably engraved with age. Before he speaks, he has already identified himself to others as a person who occupies an extreme position in the spectrum of life. Should his words and actions also betray those features we associate with advanced age, then we are further encouraged to mark him down as one who is strikingly different from ourselves.

He is also marked by numbers, of course. In the case of the elderly person, the statistics relentlessly intersect and pursue. Begin any place. Begin by tracing the declining function of this organ system or that one. Begin by measuring changes in the musculoskeletal system or the speed of central nervous system activity. Begin by locating the elderly person within the actuarial charts. Wherever we begin, it is clear the the numbers have a common bias; they are all against him.

These markings, however, do not tell the whole story. As a matter of fact, they provide only the background and props. It is true enough that any of us might contrive the story of an elderly person's life, based upon these externals. We could manufacture suppositions about what he is experiencing within these biological and statistical markings—how he regards the past, how he views the future, and all the rest. The pity of it is—we do this sort of thing much of the time, without realizing that what we are hearing is not his story, but merely the sound of our own voices. It is so easy to suppose that he feels the way we think we would feel if we were in his situation, or simply that he must feel the way we think it proper for an elderly person to feel. Any time we begin with such a

Reproduced from *Geriatrics*, August, 1969, pp. 126-133.
*Professor of Psychology, Wayne State University, Detroit, Michigan.

misstep we are likely to accumulate even further distortions. We are likely to generalize without correctives. We are likely to develop set ways of dealing with the way we think he is.

How does the elderly person actually view his own life? What is his perspective and how did he happen to develop it? What functions does it perform for him? In what ways might his perspective affect the course of his own life and the lives of others? Of his total life experiences—past, present, and potentially future—what has he included? What has he excluded? Has he settled upon this perspective as a fixed, permanent vantage point, or are other orientations to come? Most basically, has he managed to create a symbolic structure that comes to terms with his total existence at the very time that this existence itself has become so vulnerable?

To gain perspective on the life perspective of aged people, it might be helpful to back up all the way to infancy. Does the infant have a life perspective? Quite on the contrary—he is almost totally engrossed in life. He experiences the moment. He does not reexperience the past or preexperience the future, at least not in the sense which depends upon the development of symbolic structures. One of the most profound differences between infant and adult is the raw experiencing of the moment, an experiencing that lacks the protection afforded by perspective. Although this point may be an obvious one, it should be emphasized because it is important in a different light in the phenomenological world of the aged.

Very quickly, the infant comes to appreciate the difference between a presence and an absence. At first, this awareness does not distinguish between temporal and spatial dimensions. Either something (for example, smiling-mother-presenting-lunch) is both here-and-now or it is absent—totally absent. By contrast, the adult differentiates ''absence'' into several alternatives that have differential meanings to him: something exists now, but not here, in this space; or, something will be in this space at a later time; or something has been in this space, but at a previous time; or, again, something is neither here nor there, now, then, or ever.

Such distinctions, and many others that are crucial to the development of a life perspective, come later in life, but the first gropings toward a perspective begin in infancy. There is a clear directional movement. The infant becomes increasingly liberated from its biology, on the one side, and its immediate environment, on the other. The directional thrust is a general process that must be distinguished from what might be called the solidified achievements of human development. This is perhaps the most fundamental basis for challenging the notion that the aged person and the child have a great deal in common. Although certain similarities do exist, the fact remains that it is only the child who is being carried forward on the tide of psychobiological development. All of his behavior and experience is marked by the directional thrust.

The surge of general development continues with great vigor throughout the childhood years and is manifested in physical, social, and psychological changes. Although all of these developments contribute to the emergence of life perspectives, two of the most salient psychological discoveries that children make are:

1. *The discovery of futurity*. This discovery has several components. First, there is the discovery of future time in the sense that "when this moment is over, there will be some more time coming." Secondly, there is the discovery of future time as qualitatively different from any other kind of time—it is fresh, unused time that can bring forth new experiences and events. This discovery implies a dawning appreciation of possibility and uncertainty. Third, there is the discovery of world or objective future time. Implied in this discovery is the realization that one does not really possess magical control over the universe and cannot really "take time out." Additionally, this is one of the insights that prepares the child to appreciate that, for all his precious and self-evident individuality, he is simply one of many fellow creatures, all of whom dance (or drag) to the music of time.

2. *The discovery of mortality*. Some rudimentary appreciation of nonexistence may be achieved in early childhood, perhaps even before the conquest of language, but many additional years of development are required before the child can frame the concept of personal mortality. The proposition "I will die" is intimately related to the sense of futurity. It will be the continuing task of the adolescent and the adult to define the nature of this relationship for himself, to integrate the concepts of more time—fresh, new time—possibility, hope, trust, and uncertainty with the concepts of certain death.

The available evidence suggests that adolescence is usually the time during which the developing person begins seriously to create his life perspective. He has had many of the elements previously but now, for the first time, he also has the intellectual equipment to forge these elements into a perspective—and the psychosocial readiness to venture forth as his own self. Children have their notions—but it is adolescents who have ideologies. It is the transformation in thought that underlies the adolescent's changes in social behavior. He now can think about thought, compare ideal with reality, shatter the world as it is presented to him with his new tools of intellectual analysis, and at least try to put the pieces together again in a new and more satisfying manner.

Adolescence, then, is the time of life in which the act of trying to develop perspectives is dominant.

Other characteristics of adolescence are: First, the adolescent has a strong sense of moving into the future. This is not at all the same thing as planning for or visualizing the future; rather, it is a restless experiencing of the developmental current running within oneself.

Second, the adolescent typically projects his thought and feeling intensively into a fairly narrow sector of the future. It is the proximate future that counts, that decisive and eventful time which is just around the corner. Old age is so remote and unappealing a prospect that it hardly can be located at all on his projective charts.

Third, the adolescent often neglects the past, especially his personal past. Neglect may be too passive a word to describe this phenomenon. I have the impression that many adolescents are waging an active battle against the past, trying to put psychological distance between who-I-used-to-be and who-I'm-going-to-be.

Finally, there is the adolescent's way of coming to terms with finality. The prospect of death, like the prospect of aging, often is regarded as a notion that is so remote as to have no relevance to one's own life. Death is avoided, glossed over, kidded about, neutralized, and controlled by a cool, spectator type of orientation. This is on the level of what might be called self-conscious, socially communicated thought. However, more probing and indirect methods of assessment suggest that many adolescents are extremely concerned about death—both in the sense of attempting to fathom its nature and meaning and in the sense of confronting the actual prospect of their own demise. We are no longer surprised when we come across an adolescent whose behavior is influenced by the expectation that he may die at an early age. Indeed, a foreshortened life perspective is by no means the special prerogative of the aged person.

What happens to life perspective during the adult years? We know less about mature perspectives than any other sort, but I think the life perspective of a mature adult has the following characteristics:

It is, first of all, a genuine perspective. This means that the individual has been able to subdivide his life-space into multiple points which stretch away in both directions from the present moment. He is able to locate himself at any one of these points and utilize the other points to achieve the effect of perspective. He might, for example, evaluate the immediate situation in terms of its possible future consequences. A more complex perspective consists of evaluating the immediate situation in terms of both past and future circumstances. More complex still is the perspective in which the individual flexibly shifts the emphasis among past, present, and future standpoints, with all three orientations always involved but varying in relationship to each other. At one moment his pivotal concern may be with past events; thus he calls upon his immediate observations and future projections to provide a context of meaning around the past. At another moment he locates himself in the future and scans his past and present for what clues they can yield that would help him to comprehend his future self.

Upon closer inspection, his perspective will prove to be a structure that includes a variety of subperspectives. These might be visualized as operating in an umbrella type of arrangement. Opened slightly, the perspective system permits the individual to gain coverage of his proximate past and future. This could be called the yesterday-and-tomorrow framework. Opened more broadly, he now has perspective on a larger period of time, but this is still only a small range within his total life-span, where he has been and where he is going, relative to where he is now.

A mature use of the life perspective involves good judgment in deciding when it is appropriate to use a particular subperspective. It involves the ability to scan time in two distinctly different ways—the axiological and the probabilistic. In projecting future, for example, the individual identifies his hopes, fears, and values. This is the axiological orientation. But he also is capable of reading the future in a more objective style, trying to establish the most likely pattern of expectancies. The ability to sweep through time in both axiological and probabilistic styles seems to be one of the hallmarks of a mature life perspective that is maturely employed. Furthermore, there will be an optimal balance between perspectives-already-established and fresh perspective-seeking activities. A flexible life perspective makes it possible to identify and integrate the novel or unexpected event without scuttling the more enduring perspectivistic structure.

Just as important as the life perspective itself, however, is the ability to let go, to know when it is in one's best interest to become totally engrossed in a situation. All perspective and no engrossment makes for a barren, abstracted sort of life.

A mature life perspective is the type that permits a person to make constructive use of his past experiences without becoming enslaved to them and to confront his future, including the prospect of death, without capitulating in that direction either. Many people fail to develop a functional and versatile life perspective, however. In some cases we see a distorted or dysfunctional perspective; in other cases we are struck by the absence of perspective. These different psychological orientations cannot be expected to lead to the same situation when the individuals involved reach advanced age.

In exploring what has been learned and what has yet to be learned about life perspectives in the aged, we should examine the disengagement theory. This is not just a courtesy call to respect the contributions of Elaine Cumming and William E. Henry—it happens that the disengagement theory is one of the few conceptual orientations to make something of life perspectives in later adulthood. Everybody knows by now that the hypothetical process of disengagement involves a gradual and mutual withdrawal of the aging individual and his society. It is said to be an inevitable and normal developmental process. It is said to occur universally, or at least to occur universally under favorable conditions. Obviously, this is an important proposition. Is it also a true proposition? That is another question and one which would take us beyond the scope of this discussion.

But there is a relevant question here. How does the disengagement process itself get started? Cumming and Henry have suggested that disengagement begins with an event that takes place within ourselves, or more specifically, within our life perspectives. As we approach the later years of our lives we come to realize that our future is limited. There is not enough time left to do everything we had hoped and planned. Eventually we also realize that time is not only limited, but it is running out. Death comes into view as a salient prospect. Do Cumming and Henry mean that without this altered life perspective there would be no disengagement? They say: "It seems probable that disengagement would be resisted forever if there were no problem of the allocation of time and thus no anticipation of death. Questions of choice among alternative uses of time lead to curtailment of some activities. Questions of the inevitability of death lead to introspective reflections on the meaning of life."

Although this formulation emphasizes the importance of the individual's inner framework for organizing his experience and, in particular, the role of death anticipations, the formulation appears to be at variance with the facts. Although our knowledge of life perspectives is far from adequate, I believe that enough has been learned to indicate that the disengagement hypothesis has only limited application.

The disengagement hypothesis assumes that everybody has just about the same kind of perspective as they approach the later years of life. This generalization is not tenable. It is already clear that there are significant individual variations, even within particular subgroups in our own society. Some people, for example, never develop the complete umbrella of perspectives described earlier. They move through their life-span within a narrow shell of time, almost day-by-day. This kind of person does not wake up one morning and gasp, "My God, I have only a finite number of years ahead; I had best reallocate my time." The sound of distant drums never had much influence over him, and it may not get to him now, either. Many people in their seventh, eighth, and ninth decades maintain a well-entrenched narrow perspective.

By contrast, there are other people who have been brandishing a wide-open perspective umbrella ever since their youth. The use of time and the prospect of death are factors which have influenced their lives every step of the way. Such people confront different challenges than do those who may be first awakening to intimations of mortality, or those whose limited perspectives have been little influenced by the passing years.

Many people do not experience the altered outlook on time and death that Cumming and Henry proposed as the psychological trigger for disengagement, but even among those who do confront this prospect within their life perspectives, there are important variations. The disengagement theorists have stated that "The anticipation of death frees us from the obligation to participate in the ongoing stream of life. If there is only a little time left, there is no point in planning for a future and no point in putting off today's gratification."

On the contrary, many people intensify their participation in life in order to obtain the greatest possible yield from the time remaining to them. This orientation can persist well beyond the sixth and seventh decades. In studying the psychology of dying and death within a population of very aged patients in a geriatric hospital, we have encountered many who came to terms with approaching death by investing themselves solidly in the network of interpersonal life.

Furthermore, there is reason to believe that the aged person who does clamber out of "the ongoing stream of life" may be doing so for a different reason. Our research interviews suggest that in many cases the individual is not gracefully disengaging to enjoy today's gratification because the future is too short to support long-range plans. Rather, he is more likely to feel that he is no longer capable of making good use even of the limited time that is available to him. It is a sense of inner depletion, impotence, and frustration coupled with the appraisal that his environment offers very little that is inspiring or rewarding.

Perhaps Cumming and Henry have projected into the minds of elderly people the sort of outlook on time and death that they themselves believe to be reasonable and appropriate. This is one of the pitfalls of those who deal with the aged, but most aged people are not theoreticians and simply do not develop the kind of perspective that comes naturally to a theoretician's mind.

Also, we have learned from a number of aged people that they are likely to experience a double-bind regarding time—there is an awareness that future time is scarce but also a heavy sense of oppression at the hands of the clock, too much time that they cannot put to satisfying use. Even a heartfelt lament about the uselessness of future time is not identical with a will-to-die.

Finally, for at least some aged people, the qualitative nature of the future has changed radically. It is no longer the time in which exciting, fresh, novel events are to be expected. The future, in a sense, may be regarded as "used up" before it occurs. The past wends its way forward into the future.

Other points that have emerged from research and clinical experience include:

1. A foreshortened perspective at any age is likely to increase the probability of premature death. The specific pathway of lethality may be through suicide or accident, but particular attention should be given to what might be called psychosomatic or subintentional suicides, in which the individual's physical vulnerabilities are self-exploited to hasten his death.

2. The balance between perspective and engrossment becomes increasingly difficult to maintain with advanced age. An environment that truly shelters the aged person, that truly protects him during his periods of special vulnerability, would make it possible for him to enjoy the spirit-replenishing experience of engrossment more frequently. We become more vulnerable when we are engrossed. We could help our elders if we developed ways of enabling them to drop the burden of their perspectives from time to time without excessive psychological or social danger.

3. The perspective of the aged person may become more diffuse or even collapse. Changes in the direction of simplification may be appropriate and beneficial to some people. But there is the danger that the entire perspective may become dysfunctional and contribute to an unnecessarily steep decline in social integration and behavioral competency. There are things we can do that are likely to have a bolstering effect on the aged person's perspectivistic system. For example, we could enter his past as an active force, a sort of participant-observer. Too often, the aged person's preoccupation with his past chases us

away—he is snubbing us by focusing upon a scene in which we had no role. We can develop a sort of semirole in his past and, through this, help him to link his past with the present that all of us share and the future that most of us expect. We are also likely to gain something ourselves through this interpenetration of life perspectives.

4. Both our formal and informal socialization processes emphasize personal growth and expansion during the early years of life. "The System" ill prepares us for living within limits, living with losses, and living with the prospect of death. When the achievement-oriented socialization system gets to work on a person who is growing up in a deprived or ruptured environment, he is alerted to the incongruity between the ideal and the reality. His reaction may take the form of a refusal to accept the socially-sponsored perspective, in the first place, or a rapid aging of the perspective if he does try it out. The person who is growing up in an environment that makes the goals of "The System" appear attractive and feasible is, of course, more likely to develop a life perspective that is centered around individual achievement in the usual sense of the term. Both kinds of people would be better served if our socialization processes—including the classroom—offered a broader, more versatile, and more humane model from which the individual could fashion his own life perspective.

The author gratefully acknowledges the support of the University of Michigan–Wayne State University Institute of Gerontology.

THE FUNCTIONAL ASSESSMENT OF ELDERLY PEOPLE

M. Powell Lawton, Ph.D.*

Psychological testing originated in the need of school teachers to look objectively at the ability of pupils with different life experiences. Teachers were keenly aware of the biases and extraneous influences that might enter into their judgment of the educability of a youngster. Thus, Alfred Binet began to search for a standardized measure of intelligence, and originated the concept of the intelligence quotient. Although the I.Q. is going through hard times right now, the fact remains that systematic evaluation of the behavior and inner processes of the older person is an indispensable aid to the proper treatment of the aged. Techniques for assessing the functioning of older people have not yet attained the scientific sophistication of the I.Q. measurement, but they are available in a nascent form that can be of great help to the medical practitioner. This article outlines some of the rationale for assessment, with the theoretical basis, and describes some of the available techniques.

Functional assessment, in this context, means any systematic attempt to measure objectively the level at which a person is functioning, in any of a variety of areas such as physical health, quality of self-maintenance, quality of role activity, intellectual status, social activity, attitude toward the world and toward self, and emotional status. Not all these areas, strictly speaking are in the domain of mental health. However, since the unity of body and mind is nowhere better exemplified than in the aging person, it seems essential to consider every area that may possibly affect the older person's emotional state. One of the clearest and most recurrent findings in all gerontological research is the mutual inter-

Reproduced from *Journal of the American Geriatrics Society*, June, 1971, **19**, 465-481.
*Research Psychologist, Philadelphia Geriatric Center, 5301 Old York Road, Philadelphia, Pennsylvania 19141.

dependence of physical state, adaptive behavior, and emotional state. For example, in study after study, the best predictor of the morale of older people is their physical health. Thus each of the major subsystems of human function may properly be regarded as relevant to emotional health.

The busy practitioner may well wonder why he should take valuable time to use evaluational techniques. The case for formalized assessment is multifaceted:

1. Assessment insures that all areas of functioning are considered in treating the patient. In this sense, a series of devices to measure functioning in a number of different areas serves much as does a shopping list. It guards against forgetting to look at potentially important assets or liabilities. This procedure also reminds us of the strengths of the individual, as well as his weaknesses.

2. Assessment of all areas gives a more complete picture of the living, functioning person. The pattern of assets and deficits may be more significant than any specific disability. Poor mental performance in a person who is marginally competent in most other areas probably means gross general impairment. In a person whose functioning checks out well in social and instrumental areas, low mental performance may mean poor hearing, language difficulty, test anxiety, or some other nonintellectual disability.

3. Formalized assessment techniques provide some objective evidence for the clinical impression. The standardization of such measures involves much effort to achieve clarity of language, definition of terms, and instructions for questioning or rating. This somewhat compulsive exercise reduces the observer's errors and discourages bias.

4. Communication to others is facilitated. Once the spadework is done, it becomes increasingly easy to tell another member of the treatment team, or another doctor, about the patient's condition. Almost everyone has some comprehension of the meaning of a given I.Q. The physician can communicate a great deal by simply stating a cardiac patient's rating on the American Heart Association's classification system. Judicious sharing of the content of some of the assessment devices with the family may convey the magnitude of the patient's ability or disability better than can the physician's extended verbal comments.

5. The results of treatment are more easily assessed. In some cases, the patient can tell you that his symptom has disappeared, or the physician knows that the disappearance of a certain sign is clear evidence of improvement. Many disabilities have indicators that are less clear-cut, however. Physical medicine has long recognized that in order to reflect change over time in the effectiveness of functioning, small-scale measures of specific behaviors are required. Such information fed back to the physician and other members of a therapeutic team in easily communicable form is a valuable guide for what to do next. Such longitudinal measures may also positively motivate those who give treatment. If they have objective evidence that their therapy is successful, they are more likely to sustain their effort.

6. Formalized assessment helps the practitioner monitor his own professional

techniques. By looking at specific functions of his patient, he is forced to think about specific therapeutic measures that he can apply. Thus he is made aware of lacks in his own information or technical skill, and will be motivated to fill the void.

I have found it convenient to conceive of behavior in a hierarchy, ranging from relatively low complexity (the level of organ function, or disease) to the highest complexity (social behavior).[1] Inner states, in contrast, are related, but not on the same continuum.[2] In this article I discuss assessment techniques suited to each of these levels, emphasizing wherever possible those that are relatively available and easy to use by the practitioner treating older people. For most of these techniques, data are not yet at hand for establishing cut-off points to indicate what sort of action one might take. Generally, each user must establish a frame of reference in his own mind as to how low or how high a given score is for his own purposes, and for the type of patient he works with.

PHYSICAL HEALTH

There is no satisfactory global index of physical health. Health is a concept far too complex to be represented by a single number. Lawton, Ward and Yaffe[3] analyzed statistically 52 separate measures of health, hoping to obtain a smaller number of indicators. Even with the use of factor analysis to reduce the number, eight to ten separate health factors remained. It was clear that the determination of health depends upon whether one questions the subject or the doctor, or it depends upon available health records. Health behavior and health anxiety are also important aspects. The results of our factor analysis demonstrated clearly that no single index can properly represent an individual's health.

On the theory that diagnosis itself conveys some information about the subject's health, Wyler, Masuda and Holmes[4] had 117 physicians rate 126 conditions for "seriousness." They established a consensus rank order ranging from dandruff as the least serious to leukemia as the most serious. Theoretically, with this list in hand, one could sum the rankings of diagnoses pertaining to a given patient and obtain a rank sum indicating how ill he is. A still better approach, not yet established to my knowledge, would be to allow a severity rating for each condition and to sum the combined rank-times-severity ratings.

Burack,[5] in the first section of a wide-range assessment for a treatment scale, classifies chronic and acute conditions into four categories, the major dimensions being: a) relevancy to the "immediate clinical state," and b) the outlook for life expectancy. His definitions are broad enough to augment the accuracy of rating, though still concise and clear enough for ready use.

The difficulties of representing health in any unitary way have led most researchers to the easier task of measuring disability. One of the older methods of measuring disability is the Veterans Administration system of taking an individual's total functioning as a baseline, and estimating the percentage reduction in total function attributable to each diagnosed condition. Such disabilities may range from zero to 100 per cent, and are summative. Thus, a person might be considered disabled by an anxiety state to the extent that his social functioning was reduced by 20 per cent; residual pain from a shrapnel wound might occasionally be mildly exacerbated, with 10 per cent reduction in efficiency; and a burn scar would be diagnosable but not disabling. His total disability would then be 30 per cent. This system has been used successfully by the major interdisciplinary gerontology project at Duke University.[6]

Sokolow et al.[7] also have worked with percentages of disability in rating several systems, including the social and psychiatric, and combining them in *a priori* mathematical form.

Many other global measures of functional health have been used. The most global have the primary advantage of being easy to use. Conceptually they are, at best, a mixture. One such scale developed by Waldman and Fryman[8] for use at the Philadelphia Geriatric Center (PGC) is reproduced in Table 1. It is a six-point scale. The highest number under which any lettered statement is checked determines the rating. As a general guide to placement, this is a very useful scale. Among the PGC staff who know the scale, a rating of "Two" communicates a fairly accurate picture of an individual's general capability: he may need institutional care, but not necessarily in a medical setting. A patient rated "One" probably does not need such care, but a "Six" can be treated only with full hospital care.

PHYSICAL SELF-CARE

The disadvantage of global ratings is that they permit more observer bias, less directed thinking about the nature of the disability, and particularly the confusing necessity of weighing a disability in one area (a diagnosable disease, for instance) against an ability in a different area (e.g., the ability to walk normally). This is the old "peaches and pears" problem. Therefore, it is most rewarding to break down disability into its component parts, of which the ability to take care of oneself physically is the most basic. The so-called "activities of daily living schedule" (ADL) is used in most rehabilitation settings to rate objectively how independently and adequately the patient dresses, grooms himself and takes care of toileting. The tradition that each institution makes its own ADL schedule, has resulted in instruments of similar content that vary widely in psychometric sophistication.

Katz et al.[9] developed a scale that meets adequate psychometric criteria to measure whether a patient is fully dependent in bathing, dressing, going to the toilet, changing body location, feeding, and continence. They collected a great deal of validation data, and the scale is arranged in accordance with an underlying theory of physical rehabilitation. Lowenthal[10] reported a similar scale, with the advantage that independence is not an all-or-nothing measure; the scale allows for measuring degrees of dependence. Her Langley-Porter Physical Self-Maintenance Scale was modified by Lawton and Brody for easier institutional

Table 1. Physical classification

I. A. Capable of unlimited and unsupervised activity
  B. Fully ambulatory; able to go about the city independently in safety
  C. Has no physical condition requiring medical supervision or closeness to emergency medical care
  D. No evidence of heart disease in any form
  E. No evidence of prior cancer except cured skin cancer
  F. No complaints except those which cannot be related to any known disease entity

II. A. Capable of moderate activity; ambulatory without supervision for activities in his own home or immediate vicinity
  B. Can manage without help for care, and otherwise requires minimal supervision
  C. Physical condition may require medical supervision, but frequent or special treatment or closeness to medical or nursing care not required
  D. May have had a previous illness which has left no residuals, e.g., healed myocardial infarction without angina or ECG abnormalities other than healed infarctions, cancer with no evidence of recurrence, or mild diabetes (diet-controlled)

III. A. Limited capabilities
  B. Dependent on others for bedmaking and baths and general supervision of activities
  C. May or may not need a walking aid (cane) but can carry on routine activities without additional personal service
  D. Generally requires escort on the outside
  E. May require regular periodic medical care; availability of emergency medical or nursing care desirable
  F. These people have moderate incapacities such as angina, arthritis which does not limit them to a wheel-chair, chronic respiratory disease, or diabetes requiring medication

IV. A. Limited capabilities requiring assistance for personal care and daily living activities
  B. Must be in a protected environment because of need for general nursing supervision
  C. Closeness to emergency medical care desirable
  D. Requires periodic medical care at close intervals
  E. These persons are practically housebound
  F. Angina or intermittent heart disease limits physical capacities, arthritis prevents ambulation, and there are severe hearing or visual impairments, but these patients still have the capacity to be independent for daily activities after orientation

V. A. Chronically ill and confined to the vicinity of their own rooms
  B. Require a large amount of personal service, and constant supervision
  C. Should be near their own dining and toilet areas, and have a nurse on call at all times
  D. Physical condition requires 24-hour nursing care or intensive medical treatment

VI. Persons requiring hospital-type care
  A. Bed patients requiring intensive medical and nursing care
  B. Patients with infectious or contagious disease

use.[11] Table 2 shows these scales. Each scale, A through F, is checked to indicate the patient's status regarding each function. His total score may range from zero to 6, one point being given for each function in which the subject obtains the most independent score. Thus, the score communicates the general level of his self-maintaining capacity. The specifics of his abilities and disabilities are conveyed by reference to the point on each scale where his competence lies.

Table 2. Physical Self-Maintenance Scale

	Score
A. Toilet	
1. Cares for self at toilet completely; no incontinence	1
2. Needs to be reminded, or needs help in cleaning self, or has rare (weekly at most) accidents	0
3. Soiling or wetting while asleep, more than once a week	0
4. Soiling or wetting while awake, more than once a week	0
5. No control of bowels or bladder	0
B. Feeding	
1. Eats without assistance	1
2. Eats with minor assistance at meal times, with help in preparing food or with help in cleaning up after meals	0
3. Feeds self with moderate assistance and is untidy	0
4. Requires extensive assistance for all meals	0
5. Does not feed self at all and resists efforts of others to feed him	0
C. Dressing	
1. Dresses, undresses and selects clothes from own wardrobe	1
2. Dresses and undresses self, with minor assistance	0
3. Needs moderate assistance in dressing or selection of clothes	0
4. Needs major assistance in dressing but cooperates with efforts of others to help	0
5. Completely unable to dress self and resists efforts of others to help	0
D. Grooming (neatness, hair, nails, hands, face, clothing)	
1. Always neatly dressed and well-groomed, without assistance	1
2. Groom self adequately, with occasional minor assistance, e.g., in shaving	0
3. Needs moderate and regular assistance or supervision in grooming	0
4. Needs total grooming care, but can remain well groomed after help from others	0
5. Actively negates all efforts of others to maintain grooming	0
E. Physical ambulation	
1. Goes about grounds or city	1
2. Ambulates within residence or about one block distant	0
3. Ambulates with assistance of (check one): a ( ) another person, b( ) railing, c ( ) cane, d ( ) walker, or e ( ) wheelchair:	0
(1) Gets in and out without help	
(2) Needs help in getting in and out	
4. Sits unsupported in chair or wheelchair, but cannot propel self without help	0
5. Bedridden more than half the time	0
F. Bathing	
1. Bathes self (tub, shower, sponge bath) without help	1
2. Bathes self, with help in getting in and out of tub	0
3. Washes face and hands only, but cannot bathe rest of body	0
4. Does not wash self but is cooperative with those who bathe him	0
5. Does not try to wash self, and resists efforts to keep him clean	0

Norms usable for individual decision-making do not exist yet. however, rough guidelines may be found in data from 343 cases; in this series, applicants to a home for aged had a mean score of 4.1, patients admitted to a mental hospital reception center had a mean score of 3.5, and protective-custody patients had a mean score of 2.0. Thus, a zero score would probably preclude adjustment outside an institution which provides very close supervision, but a score in the range 2-6 would allow placement in a home for the aged (depending upon the amount of service available).

INSTRUMENTAL ACTIVITIES OF DAILY LIVING

Paid work is the best example of an instrumental activity. After retirement, other daily tasks become most relevant to the living of a minimally adequate social life. Lawton and Brody[11] named a set of eight such tasks the Instrumental Activities of Daily Living (IADL) as shown in Table 3. One can live outside an institution without being able to perform some of them satisfactorily. However, the more these abilities are impaired, the more will formal or family-administered services be required to maintain the person in the community. The IADL is also scaled as in the self-maintenance scale, but in the IADL, a person receives a score of 1 for each item labelled A through H if his competence attains some minimal level *or higher*. Thus, for item A, telephone use, the subject receives one tally if he can answer the telephone, or do better; on item B, however, he gets a tally only if he can take care of all shopping needs independently. Items C and D (cooking and housekeeping) are relatively specific to the female role and are therefore not included in scoring for males. We have tested fewer subjects on this scale than are requisite for even minimal use for screening, and therefore recommend that each user treat the scale qualitatively at first, until he gets some idea of how his own patients are responding. The examiner fills out the scale on the basis of the maximal amount of knowledge he has about the patient from the patient himself, informants, and recent records.

MENTAL STATUS

Mental status in its traditional usage refers to the capacity to be oriented for time, place and person, to remember, and to perform intellectual tasks of varying degrees of difficulty. Traditional psychological testing with standardized tests such as the Wechsler Adult Intelligence Scale are the most satisfactory measures of mental status, provided the person is attentive, educated at least to a minimal level, conversant in English, unimpaired in senses, and accepts the testing situation as one worth his cooperation. These provisos eliminate many elderly subjects; moreover, the services of a psychologist are not always available. Also, the task is frequently one of discriminating between severe mental impairment and moderate impairment, which cannot be accomplished with many of the standardized tests. To meet this need, Kahn, Pollack and Goldfarb[12] designed the ten-item Mental Status Questionnaire (MSQ) shown in Table 4. With

Table 3. Scale for Instrumental Activities of Daily Living

Males' score		Females' score
	A. Ability to use telephone	
1	1. Operates telephone on own initiative; looks up and dials numbers, etc.	1
1	2. Dials a few well-known numbers	1
1	3. Answers telephone but does not dial	1
0	4. Does not use telephone at all	0
	B. Shopping	
1	1. Takes care of all shopping needs independently	1
0	2. Shops independently for small purchases	0
0	3. Needs to be accompanied on any shopping trip	0
0	4. Completely unable to shop	0
	C. Food preparation	
	1. Plans, prepares and serves adequate meals independently	1
	2. Prepares adequate meals if supplied with ingredients	0
	3. Heats and serves prepared meals, or prepares meals but does not maintain adequate diet	0
	4. Needs to have meals prepared and served	0
	D. Housekeeping	
	1. Maintains house alone or with occasional assistance (e.g., heavy-work domestic help)	1
	2. Performs light daily tasks such as dish-washing and bed-making	1
	3. Performs light daily tasks but cannot maintain acceptable level of cleanliness	1
	4. Needs help with all home maintenance tasks	1
	5. Does not participate in any housekeeping tasks	0
	E. Laundry	
	1. Does personal laundry completely	1
	2. Launders small items; rinses socks, stockings, etc.	1
	3. All laundry must be done by others	0
	F. Mode of transportation	
1	1. Travels independently on public transportation or drives own car	1
1	2. Arranges own travel via taxi, but does not otherwise use public transportation	1
0	3. Travels on public transportation when assisted or accompanied by another	1
0	4. Travel limited to taxi or automobile, with assistance of another	0
0	5. Does not travel at all	0
	G. Responsibility for own medication	
1	1. Is responsible for taking medication in correct dosages at correct time	1
0	2. Takes responsibility if medication is prepared in advance in separate dosages	0
0	3. Is not capable of dispensing own medication	0
	H. Ability to handle finances	
1	1. Manages financial matters independently (budgets, writes checks, pays rent and bills, goes to bank); collects and keeps track of income	1
1	2. Manages day-to-day purchases, but needs help with banking, major purchases, etc.	1
0	3. Incapable of handling money	0

Table 4. Mental Status Questionnaire

1. Where are we now? (Correct name of place)	8. What year were you born?
2. Where is this place? (Correct city)	9. Who is President of the United States?
3. What is today's *date?* (Day of month)	10. Who was President before him?
4. What month is it?	Scores: 0-2 CBS absent or mild
5. What year is it?	3-8 CBS moderate
6. How old are you?	9-10 CBS severe
7. What is your birthday? (Month)	

such a simple series of items, the examiner can compensate for the subject's deficiencies in language, sensory reception, attention, or motivation by mechanisms such as repetition, speaking loudly, translating, and working hard to mobilize the subject's attention for a brief span of time. The authors have tested enough people with this questionnaire to be able to identify the gradations of probable chronic brain syndrome noted in Table 4. Independent psychiatric examinations of 328 subjects indicated that only 12 per cent of older patients making no errors or only 1 or 2 errors were certifiable as suffering from mental illness by New York State standards, whereas 78 per cent of those making 9 or 10 errors were certifiable. This MSQ is in wide use as an aid to understanding just how much of a patient's exhibited difficulty is attributable to chronic brain syndrome. "Normal" senescence does not result in a lowering of scores on the MSQ, nor do most neurotic conditions. Nonorganic psychoses (depression, schizophrenia) may or may not result in lowered scores, but other indicators can usually determine whether it is a functional psychosis that is impairing performance.

There are many other approaches to the assessment of functional mental status. The MSQ will not discriminate above a minimal level of competence. However, the physician in practice is less likely to have to distinguish whether his older patient is superior or only average in intelligence. Such a question may be relevant in extended counseling, vocational redirection, or psychiatric rehabilitation. In these instances, a complete series of psychodiagnostic tests should be performed by a clinical psychologist.

SOCIAL ROLES AND ACTIVITIES

The more complex the behavior, the more difficult it is to measure successfully. Social behavior on a very low level can be measured fairly accurately, as in the author's[13] adaptation of a Minimal Social Behavior Scale (MSBS).[14] This test situation presents the subject with a number of basic social stimuli (such as a greeting, an invitation to be seated, a chance to do a favor, and so on), and the responses are scored for their social appropriateness. Table 5 shows the 25-item geriatric version of the MSBS. Norms are not available for this test, but a rough idea of how scores run may be gained from the fact that the average score for relatively intact geriatric mental patients was 22, whereas the average score for impaired and uncooperative patients was 15.

Table 5. Minimal Social Behavior Scale

A. E. goes to S. and introduces himself: *"I am _____, Mrs. _____. I'm glad to meet you,"* extending hand.
  1. Score + if any discernible response to greeting
  2. Score + if response is verbal and appropriate
  3. Score + if S, offers hand to E.

B. E. says either (a) *"Won't you have a seat?"* or (b) *"May I sit with you for a while?"* depending on whether S. is brought to E. or E. comes to S.
  4. Score + if (a) S. sits without urging, or (b) S. assents or acknowledges E.'s comment

C. E. says *"How are you today?"*
  5. Score + if any discernible response to question
  6. Score + if response is verbal and appropriate

D. E. drops pencil by pushing it off desk, ostensibly by accident. If S. does not pick up pencil spontaneously, E. says *"Would you pick up the pencil for me?"*
  7. Score + if S. picks up pencil at all
  8. Score + if S. picks up pencil spontaneously

E. E. says *"I have something I want to show you."* E. holds in front of S., Figure A of the Bender-Gestalt test (E. may draw for S. a circle being touched by one corner of a square).
  9. Score + if S. looks at Bender card

F. *"Here is a pencil."* E. offers it to S., puts paper in front of S., and says, *"I would like you to copy this drawing on this paper."*
  10. Score + if S. accepts pencil without further urging
  11. Score + if S. makes any mark on paper
  12. Score + if S. draws an appropriate circle and 4-sided figure

G. E. says *"How are you getting along?"*
  13. Score + if any discernible response to the question
  14. Score + if the response is verbal and appropriate

H. E. crumples a scrap of paper and tosses it at a wastebasket previously placed next to S., purposely missing.
  15. Score + if S. spontaneously picks up paper and deposits it in wastebasket

I. E. says *"I have a few questions I would like to ask you."* (E. administers questions 1-10 of Kahn-Goldfarb Mental Status Questionnaire.)
  16. Score + if S. makes any verbal response, irrespective of content, to all questions 1-10.

J. E. places a magazine in front of S. and busies himself with writing on pad while saying, *"I'll be busy a minute."*
  17. Score + if S. turns at least one page of magazine

K. E. rises and extends hand, saying *"Thank you very much Mr(s). _____."*
  18. Score + if S. acknowledges E.'s departure either verbally or with gesture

L. The remainder of the items are based on E.'s judgment of the behavior of the patient throughout the interview:
  19. Score + unless inappropriate grimaces or mannerisms are readily apparent
  20. Score + if the patient at any time looks E. in the eye
  21. Score + unless S. obviously appears to avoid E.'s gaze at all times, or stares at E. fixedly
  22. Score + unless S. sits in a bizarre position or is in constant motion or nearly motionless
  23. Score + unless S.'s clothes are obviously disarranged, unbuttoned, or misbuttoned
  24. Score + unless S. is drooling or nasal mucus is visible or food deposits are conspicuous on clothes or face
  25. Score + unless S. attempts to move away from E. before termination of interview with explanation

---

For behavior within the normal range, the most-used instrument over the years has been the Chicago Activity and Attitude Inventory.[15] The first part of this inventory obtains information on the subject's behavior in the areas of health, friendship and family contacts, leisure-time use, economic security, and religion. The inventory is out of print, but may be reproduced from the book; information on the manual, with norms for large numbers of older people, may be obtained from its author.* With these norms, one can compare a given older person's level of activity with that of other people roughly comparable in status to the subject. The one major difficulty with the Inventory is that it is set up in "test" format, so that the subject fills out his own responses. Both the test format and the language in which the items are phrased are likely to cause some response problems in older people below a moderate level of sophistication and mental competence.

Havighurst has also developed a set of Role Activity Ratings by which an informant or professional who knows the subject well can rate activity in a number of relatively specific roles such as grandparent, parent, extended family member, business club member, or civic participant. In one form, the level of competence with which the subject performs the role tasks is rated.[16] In the other and slightly more extended form, the energy expended in the role behavior, rather than its quality, is rated.[17] Norms for the latter are available for older people in several countries.

ATTITUDES, MORALE, AND LIFE SATISFACTION

On the level of inner psychological state, the usual standard assessment instruments such as the Minnesota Multiphasic Personality Inventory, the Edwards Personal Preference Schedule, or the Maudsley Personality Inventory are quite unsuitable for many geriatric patients. They are too long, and the language of even the simplest of them (the MMPI) taxes the comprehension of enough patients to preclude their routine use. Because of these difficulties, a number of scales have been designed specifically for older people. There is not enough space here to discuss adequately and to distinguish among the concepts of attitudes, morale, life satisfaction, adjustment, and positive mental health in older people. Excellent considerations of these issues have been presented by Rosow[18] and Havighurst,[19] and a review of some work in this area was made by Lawton.[20]

One approach to the measurement of attitude is that of Cavan et al.—the Chicago Activity and Attitude Inventory.[15] The section of activities described above is followed by a section in which the subject is asked questions regarding his attitudes and satisfaction with each major field activity.

The simplest measure of morale, and one that has been found useful in a large

*Robert Havighurst, Ph.D., Judd Hall, University of Chicago, Chicago, Illinois 60637.

Table 6. Kutner Morale Scale

Question	Response alternatives	Score
1. How often do you feel that there's just no point in living—often, sometimes, or hardly ever?	Often	0
	Sometimes	0
	Hardly ever	1
2. Things just keep getting worse and worse for me as I get older	Agree	0
	Disagree	1
3. How much do you regret the chances you missed during your life to do a better job of living—not at all, somewhat, or a good deal?	Not at all	1
	Somewhat	0
	A good deal	0
4. All in all, how much unhappiness would you say you find in life today?—almost none; some, but not very much; a good deal?	Almost none	1
	Some, but not very much	0
	A good deal	0
5. On the whole, how satisfied would you say you are with your way of life today? Would you say—very satisfied, fairly satisfied, or not very satisfied?	Very satisfied	1
	Fairly satisfied	0
	Not very satisfied	0
6. How much do you plan ahead the things you will be doing next week or the week after? Would you say you make—many plans, a few plans, or almost none?	Many plans	1
	A few plans	1
	Almost none	0
7. As you get older, would you say things seem to be better or worse than you thought they would be?	Better	1
	Worse	0
	Same	0

Scores: 0-2 Low morale
3-4 Medium
5-6 High morale

number of gerontological studies, is the Kutner Morale Scale, shown in Table 6.[21] The subject receives one tally for each item answered in the direction indicated in Table 6. Among the 500 subjects of Kutner et al., approximately one-third each received scale scores classifiable as high, medium, and low respectively. This scale can be read and answered by the subject, or an examiner can read him the questions. Its brevity makes the Kutner scale an admirable instrument for brief assessment. However, its content is limited, its language ponderous, and its brevity a liability in terms of its capacity to measure accurately a complex concept.

Neugarten, Havighurst and Tobin,[22] in connection with the Kansas City Study of Adult Life,[23] assembled a set of questions that seemed central for adjustment to living during old age. Using information obtained from depth psychological interviews as a validating criterion, they painstakingly devised two measures of adjustment: 1) Life Satisfaction Index A, and 2) Life Satisfaction

Table 7. Life Satisfaction Index Z

	Score		
	Agree	**?**	**Disagree**
1. As I grow older, things seem better than I thought they would be	2	1	0
2. I have gotten more breaks in life than most of the people I know	2	1	0
3. This is the dreariest time of my life	0	1	2
4. I am just as happy as when I was younger	2	1	0
5. These are the best years of my life	2	1	0
6. Most of the things I do are boring or monotonous	0	1	2
7. The things I do are as interesting to me as they ever were	2	1	0
8. As I look back on my life, I am fairly well satisfied	2	1	0
9. I have made plans for things I'll be doing a month or a year from now	2	1	0
10. When I think back over my life, I didn't get most of the important things I wanted	0	1	2
11. Compared to other people, I get down in the dumps too often	0	1	2

Index B. The former scale has been analyzed further and its length reduced to 13 items, as shown in Table 7—the Life Satisfaction Index Z.[24] Among the normal aged, Wood, Wylie, and Sheafor[24] found that scores of 0-12 indicated low morale, 13-21 moderate, and 22-26 high morale. Norms are not available for many groups, however, such as psychiatric patients, and the user must again establish his own frame of reference. The longer version may be reproduced from the original article,[22] and studies using a variety of types of aged people have been reported.

Lawton was dissatisfied with the language, the sometimes difficult response format, and the lack of comprehensiveness of content of other measures of morale, and assembled a group of items with these considerations in mind.[20] The items found to be valid predictors of rated adjustment were subjected to a factor analysis, resulting in the Philadelphia Geriatric Center Morale Scale shown in Table 8. A total score is obtained by summing all the "plus" responses. The average score obtained by 500 tenants of specialized housing developments for the elderly was about 13. Scores ranging from 10 through 17 can be considered usual, whereas scores of 9 or below raise a distinct question as to whether the person is in some psychological distress, or badly mismatched with his total environmental situation. The PGC Morale Scale deliberately phrases questions in an oversimplified way, and forces responses into an "either-or" format so as to be easy for almost everyone to answer. It may be filled out by the subject himself, or read and marked by an examiner. The results of the statistical analysis (not presented here) indicated that the test was successful in measuring diverse aspects of morale, such as anxiety, loneliness, pessimistic

Table 8. Philadelphia Geriatric Center (PGC) Morale Scale

Question	Response alternatives	Score
1. Things keep getting worse as I get older	No	1
	Yes	0
2. I have as much pep as I did last year	Yes	1
	No	0
3. How much do you feel lonely?	Not much	1
	A lot	0
4. Little things bother me more this year	Yes	0
	No	1
5. I see enough of my friends and relatives	Yes	1
	No	0
6. As you get older you are less useful	Yes	0
	No	1
7. If you could live where you wanted, where would you live?		"Here" is the only +
8. I sometimes worry so much that I can't sleep	No	1
	Yes	0
9. As I get older, things are better, worse, or the same as I thought they would be	Better	1
	Worse	0
	Same	0
10. I sometimes feel that life isn't worth living	Yes	0
	No	1
11. I am as happy now as I was when I was younger	Yes	1
	No	0
12. I have a lot to be sad about	No	1
	Yes	0
13. People had it better in the old days	Yes	0
	No	1
14. I am afraid of a lot of things	Yes	0
	No	1
15. I get mad more than I used to	No	1
	Yes	0
16. Life is hard for me most of the time	Yes	0
	No	1
17. How satisfied are you with your life today?	Not satisfied	0
	Satisfied	1
18. I take things hard	No	1
	Yes	0
19. A person has to live for today and not worry about tomorrow	No	0
	Yes	1
20. My health is the same, better, or worse than most people my age	Better	1
	Same	1
	Worse	0
21. I get upset easily	No	1
	Yes	0

outlook, dissatisfaction with the environment, and negative attitude toward aging.

PSYCHIATRIC STATUS

There are, by now, hundreds of formal devices for rating psychiatric status from a pathology-oriented point of view. A number of these can be used with the aged, but few have been designed specifically with the common symptoms of this group in mind. This lack is almost complete in the case of formalized psychiatric ratings designed for the patient living in the community. Most of the schedules now in use are, unfortunately, designed with the institutionalized patient in mind. The best of these is very long and still in an experimental stage —the Mental Status Schedule, Geriatric Supplement, of Spitzer et al.[25] All aspects of psychiatric symptomatology, thinking, and social behavior are covered in this schedule. With appropriate training it may be completed by observers who are not psychiatrists.* One of the better ward behavior rating scales, the Stockton Rating Scale, was devised by Meer and Baker expressly for the geriatric patient.[26] In addition to the usual items dealing with deficits in physical self-maintenance, the 33 items contain scales for apathy, communication failure, and socially irritating behavior. However, in consideration of the fact that instrument development in this area is in such an early stage, it may be preferable to rely on the usual clinical psychiatric evaluation if a general noninstitutional assessment of psychiatric status is desired.

COMMENT

The availability of specific measures of functioning in these different areas makes it relatively easy to get a picture of how a specific older person compares with other elderly people. The entire set of functions might not necessarily have to be tested in order to arrive at some treatment-relevant conclusions. In any case, the procedures would act as a skeleton for the total clinical assessment. None of them is precise enough to be used rigidly, with cut-off points for decision-making. However, clinical decisions made with the assistance of these formal devices may be a distinct improvement over those made solely on the basis of "clinical feel."

---

*Information on Mental Status Schedule forms, administration and scoring may be obtained from Biometrics Research, 722 W. 168 St., New York, N.Y. 10032.

REFERENCES

1. Lawton, M. P.: Assessing the competence of older people, in Kent, D., Kastenbaum, R. and Sherwood, S. (Eds.): Research, Planning, and Action for the Elderly. New York, Behavioral Publications (in press).
2. Lawton, M. P.: Problems in functional assessment. Paper presented at the Annual Meeting of the Gerontological Society, Denver, Colorado. November 1968.
3. Lawton, M. P.; Ward, M., and Yaffe, S.: Indices of health in an aging population, J. Gerontol. **22:**334, 1967.

4. Wyler, A. R.; Masuda, M., and Holmes, T. H.: Seriousness of illness rating scale, J. Psychosom. Res. **11:**363, 1968.
5. Burack, B.: Interdisciplinary classification for the aged, J. Chron. Dis. **18:**1059, 1965.
6. Maddox, G.: Self-assessment of health status, J. Chron. Dis. **17:**449, 1964.
7. Sokolow, J.; Silson, J.; Taylor, E.; Anderson, E., and Rusk, H.: A new approach to the objective evaluation of physical disability, J. Chron. Dis. **15:**105, 1962.
8. Waldman, A., and Fryman, E.: Classification in homes for the aged, in Shore, H. and Leeds, M. (Eds.): Geriatric Institutional Management. New York, Putnam, 1964, pp. 131-135.
9. Katz, S.; Downs, T. D.; Cash, H. R., and Grotz, R. C.: Progress in development of the index of ADL, Gerontologist **10:**20, 1970 (Part I).
10. Lowenthal, M. F.: Lives in Distress. New York, Basic Books, 1964.
11. Lawton, M. P., and Brody, E.: Assessment of older people: self-maintaining and instrumental activities of daily living. Gerontologist **9:**179, 1969.
12. Kahn, R. L.; Pollack, M., and Goldfarb, A. I.: Factors related to individual differences in mental status of institutionalized aged. New York State Department of Mental Hygiene, Office for Aging. (Mimeo report, undated.)
13. Lawton, M. P.: Schizophrenia forty-five years later, J. Genet. Psychol. (in press).
14. Farina, A.; Arenberg, D., and Guskin, S.: A scale for measuring minimal social behavior, J. Consult. Psychol. **21:**265, 1957.
15. Caven, R. S.; Burgess, E. W.; Havighurst, R. J., and Goldhamer, H.: Personal Adjustment in Old Age. Chicago, Science Research Associates, 1949.
16. Havighurst, R.: The social competence of middle-aged people, Genet. Psychol. Monogr. **56:**297, 1957.
17. Havighurst, R. J.; Munnichs, J. M. A.; Neugarten, B. L., and Thomae, H.: Adjustment to Retirement—A Cross-National Study. New York, Humanities Press, 1969.
18. Rosow, I.: Adjustment of the normal aged, in Williams, R. H., Tibbitts, C. and Donahue, W. (Eds.): Processes of Aging, Volume II. New York, Atherton, 1963, pp. 195-223.
19. Havighurst, R.: Successful aging, in Williams, R. H., Tibbitts, C. and Donahue, W. (Eds.): Processes of Aging, Volume I. New York, Atherton, 1963, pp. 299-320.
20. Lawton, M. P.: The dimensions of morale, in Kent, D., Kastenbaum, R. and Sherwood, S. (Eds.): Research, Planning, and Action for the Elderly. New York, Behavioral Publications (in press).
21. Kutner, B; Fanshel, D.; Togo, A. M., and Langner, T. S.: Five Hundred Over Sixty. New York, Russell Sage Foundation, 1956.
22. Neugarten, B. L.; Havighurst, R. J., and Tobin, S. S.: The measurement of life satisfaction, J. Gerontol. **16:**134, 1961.
23. Cumming, E., and Henry, W.: Growing Old. New York, Basic Books, 1961.
24. Wood, V.; Wylie, M. L., and Sheafor, B.: An analysis of a short self-report measure of life satisfaction: correlation with rater judgments, J. Gerontol. **24:**465, 1969.
25. Spitzer, R. L.; Burdock, E. I.; Endicott, J.; Cohen, G. M.; Bennett, R., and Weinstock, C.: Mental Status Schedule, Geriatric Supplement. Biometrics Research, New York State Department of Mental Hygiene, New York City, 1966.
26. Meer, B., and Baker, J. A.: The Stockton Geriatric Rating Scale, J. Gerontol. **21:**392, 1966.

THE EFFECTS OF AGING
ON ACTIVITIES AND ATTITUDES*

Erdman B. Palmore, Ph.D.**

Does aging reduce activities and attitudes? Most cross-sectional surveys agree that it does, but recent longitudinal evidence tends to question the extent of this reduction. Are decreases in activities related to decreases in satisfaction? Disengagement theory maintains that high satisfaction in aging results from acceptance of the "inevitable" reduction in interaction, while "activity theory" maintains that reduction in activity results in reduction of satisfaction. Is there a persistence of life style among the aged? There is evidence that, regardless of the average effects of aging, individual persons tend to maintain relatively high or relatively low levels of activity and satisfaction during their later years. Does aging increase homogeneity or differentiation? Again, theories have been advanced supporting both positions.

Such questions and theories have fascinated social gerontologists for at least the two decades since the Chicago group developed their Activity and Attitude Inventory (Cavan, Burgess, Havighurst, and Goldhamer, 1949). A major reason for the uncertain answers and conflicting theories is that usually cross-sectional data were used even though these questions deal with change over time. It was not until 1963 that longitudinal data were first presented in an attempt to clarify these uncertainties (Maddox, 1963). The present paper discusses new longitudi-

Reproduced from *The Gerontologist,* Winter, 1968, **8,**259-263.

*The research on which this paper is based was supported in part by Grant HD-00668, National Institute of Child Health and Human Development, USPHS. The computations involved were carried out in the Duke University Computing Laboratory, which is supported in part by the National Science Foundation. Programming for the computations was done by Mrs. Nancy Watson.

**Center for the Study of Aging and Human Development, Duke University, Durham, North Carolina 27706.

nal findings relevant to these questions from data that now cover a ten-year period of tests and retests.

METHODS

One hundred twenty-seven (out of 256) volunteer participants in a longitudinal, interdisciplinary study of aging were examined and interviewed the first time during 1955-1959 and were reinterviewed at approximately three-year intervals so that they had completed four waves of interviews by 1966-1967.* When interviewed the fourth time, they ranged in age from 70 to 93 with a mean age of 78. Fifty-one were men and 76 were women. There was less than one year's difference between the mean age for men and the mean age for women. All were ambulatory, noninstitutionalized residents of the central North Carolina area. The initial panel of 256 persons did not constitute a random sample of Durham residents, but were chosen from a larger number of volunteers so that their sex, racial, and occupational distribution approximated that of the area. Nevertheless, analysis of selection and attrition factors indicates that the panelists were a social, psychological, and physical elite among the aged and became more so through time (Maddox, 1962). However, since longitudinal analysis uses each S as his own control and examines changes over time rather than comparing younger with older Ss, the degree to which the sample of an age category represents the universe of an age category is a less critical issue than in cross-sectional studies.

We need not discuss here the various advantages of longitudinal analysis for studying aging, such as its greater sensitivity and its ability to measure change directly rather than inferentially (Goldfarb, 1960; Maddox, 1965), but we might point out one advantage of repeated measurements that has not been widely recognized. This is the ability to use consistency as a test of reliable and significant change when one has three or more repeated measurements on the same sample. When a change is observed between two points in time, there is always the possibility that this change might be due to temporary or chance fluctuations. But when the same change is observed between the second and third points in time, our confidence in the reliability and significance of this change can be greatly increased because the probability of two such changes occurring by chance is much smaller. Thus, in the present discussion we shall focus on consistent changes (or lack of consistency) as well as on the statistically significant changes.

The Inventory of Activity and Attitudes questions were read to the Ss by a social worker as part of a longer social history. The Activity Inventory consists of 20 questions dealing with five areas of activities (about four questions for each area): health (physical capacity to act); family and friends (frequency of contacts); leisure (ways of spending time, hobbies, reading, organizations);

---

*A few Ss missed the second or third wave of interviews but all 127 returned for the fourth wave.

economic (amount of work or housework and lack of economic restrictions on activity); and religious activity (attendance at religious services, listening to them on radio or TV, reading religious literature).* Each sub-score could range from zero to ten with the higher scores indicating more activity. The total activity score is the sum of the sub-scores in these five areas (total range: 0-50).

The Attitude Inventory consists of 56 agree-disagree items about the S's satisfaction with eight areas of his life (seven items in each area): health, friends, work, economic security, religion, usefulness, family, and general happiness.† The score in each area could range from zero to six (one item of the seven is neutral in the scoring) with the higher scores indicating more satisfaction. The total attitude score is the sum of the scores in these eight areas (total range: 0-48). Further discussion of the development, purpose, scoring, reliability, and validity of these inventories may be found in Cavan et al. (1949) and Havighurst (1951). These inventories have been used in more than 20 different studies and the results show a relatively high degree of reliability and validity.

As a check on the Inventory of Activity and Attitudes, the social worker interviewing the Ss used the Cavan Adjustment Rating Scale to give her estimation of the Ss' activities and attitudes (Havighurst and Albrecht, 1953). In general, the results from these scales were similar to those from the Activity and Attitude Inventory.

Some may question the appropriateness of comparing mean scores and correlations on the grounds that such analysis assumes equal intervals in the scales even though we are not sure this assumption is justified. However, several statisticians have recently pointed out that treating ordinal scales as equal-interval scales (1) involves assumptions that may be no more misleading than the use of arbitrary cutpoints that obscure differences in amount of variation (Blalock, 1961); (2) has been useful in developing more accurate measurements and theory in most sciences (Burke, 1963); (3) usually involves relatively little error (Labovitz, 1967); and in general allows much more powerful and sensitive analysis. Since we are interested primarily in direction of change and relative changes rather than absolute amounts of change, this type of analysis seems worth the risk of assuming equal intervals.

RESULTS

Small reductions. The men had almost no over-all reduction over the ten years in either activities or attitudes (Tables 1 and 2). The women had significant but quite small (less than 7%) reductions in both activities and attitudes. This

---

*Typical questions: How many days did you spend in bed last year? How often do you see some of your family or close relatives? How many club meetings do you usually attend each month? Are you working now (full-time, part-time, or not working)? How often do you attend religious services?
† Typical items: I feel just miserable most of the time. I have all the good friends anyone could wish. I am satisfied with the work I now do. I am just able to make ends meet. Religion is a great comfort to me. My life is meaningless now. I am perfectly satisfied with the way my family treats me. My life is full of worry.

Table 1. Mean activity scores at four points in time

Activities	Time 1	Time 2	Time 3	Time 4
Men				
Health	2.4	3.9*	3.1	2.6
Family and friends	6.8	7.5	6.8	6.9
Leisure	6.9	5.8*	5.7*	5.6*
Economic	4.8	4.9	5.3	6.0
Religious	6.3	6.1	5.5	6.0
Total	27.2	28.2	26.4	27.1
Women				
Health	2.5	3.2	2.6	2.5
Family and friends	5.9	6.1	5.5	5.3*
Leisure	7.7	7.2	6.6*	6.3*
Economic	7.4	7.5	8.1	8.4*
Religious	6.7	7.1	6.4	6.7
Total	30.2	31.1	29.2*	29.2*

*Difference between this score and score at Time 1 is significant at .01 level according to the *t*-test for paired observations.

Table 2. Mean attitude scores at four points in time

Attitudes	Time 1	Time 2	Time 3	Time 4
Men				
Health	3.8	3.7	4.1	3.5
Friends	4.6	4.4	4.3	4.2
Work	3.7	3.6	3.8	3.4
Economic security	3.3	3.6	4.0*	3.7
Religion	5.2	5.3	5.3	5.5*
Usefulness	4.3	4.3	4.3	4.0
Family	4.9	4.6	4.9	5.0
Happiness	4.3	4.4	3.6*	4.1
Total	34.1	33.9	34.3	33.4
Women				
Health	4.0	3.8	3.7	3.6*
Friends	4.5	4.4	4.5	4.3
Work	3.9	3.8	3.7	3.5*
Economic security	3.8	3.9	4.0*	4.0*
Religion	5.5	5.6	5.7*	5.6
Usefulness	4.6	4.3	4.4	4.1*
Family	4.7	4.8	4.9	4.8
Happiness	4.2	4.1	3.6*	3.6*
Total	35.2	34.7	34.5*	33.5*

*Difference between this score and score at Time 1 is significant at .01 level according to the *t*-test for paired observations.

Table 3. Correlations (r) of changes in activities with changes in total attitudes (Time 1 to Time 4)

Activity	Men	Women
Health	.07	.09
Family and friends	.12	.27*
Leisure	.22	.10
Economic	.36*	.30*
Religious	.26	.13
Total activity	.42*	.40*

*The probability of this correlation occurring by chance is less than .01.

lack of substantial reduction in activities is contrary to disengagement theory which asserts that marked withdrawal from activities is the modal pattern in aging (Cumming and Henry, 1961). It is also contrary to the findings of most cross-sectional surveys (for example, Havighurst and Albrecht, 1953) and contrary to the commonly held assumption that most people become less active as they age. On the other hand, it is consistent with previous longitudinal findings from this panel (Maddox, 1963) (Table 3).

There are two plausible explanations for this apparent contradiction. While the aged may disengage or reduce activities in *some* areas such as belonging to organizations and attending meetings (as shown by the declining leisure activities scores) or retiring from work (most of our panel was already retired), they may compensate by increasing activities in other areas such as contacts with family and friends or reading religious literature. Or a temporary decrease may be compensated for by a subsequent increase. Or some may reduce while others increase. The net effect would then be little or no change in the average total activities score. Second, this panel represents those relatively healthy aged who were community residents and who survived for over ten years from the first wave to their fourth wave, "ripe old age," of 70 to 93. It may be that the relatively healthy aged do maintain a fairly stable plateau of activity up until just before death and that it is only the ill or disabled aged who pull the average activity level down in cross-sectional studies. The cross-sectional association of poor health and low activity is well established (Jeffers and Nichols, 1961; Havighurst and Albrecht, 1953). The same explanations would apply to the mixed changes in attitudes which show some increases, some decreases, and no significant net decrease in total attitudes among men.

It is unlikely that this pattern of small or insignificant decreases could be attributed to unreliability in the tests, because the reliability of these tests has been demonstrated elsewhere and is confirmed in this study by the moderately high correlations of earlier scores with later scores (Table 4).

The fact that women had larger and more consistent decreases in both activities and attitudes seems to indicate that aging produces greater net changes

Table 4. Correlations (r) of earlier score with later score for total activities and total attitudes

Variable	Time 1 with Time 2	Time 2 with Time 3	Time 3 with Time 4	Time 1 with Time 4
Men				
Total activities	.57	.57	.46	.27
Total attitudes	.74	.73	.71	.65
Women				
Total activities	.75	.65	.74	.60
Total attitudes	.67	.66	.79	.56

for women than men, at least in this age range. This may be related to the fact that most of the men had already retired before the beginning of this study and thus did not have to adjust to that change in status during the course of the study. Indeed, their increasing economic activity scores indicate that many men went back to work or increased their work during the study.

The small but significant increases of interest in religion, despite no increase in religious activities, confirm the findings of the cross-sectional studies (Moberg, 1965). This has been related to approaching death and increasing concern with after-life. However, Havighurst (1951) found that religious attitudes had practically no correlations with the total scores nor with the other sub-scores. He suggested that, since the religious items seemed to be measuring a different kind of dimension from the rest of the attitude scale, they should not be included in the total score. We also found that the religious attitude scores had almost no correlation with the total attitude score at any point in time (most of the correlations were less than .15) and that many of the correlations with the other subscores were even negative. We agree with Havighurst that the religion items should be dropped or considered separately from the rest of the attitude scale.

Activity correlates with attitudes. Changes in total activities were significantly and positively correlated with changes in total attitudes (Table 3). This means that those who reduced their activities as they aged tended to suffer reduction in over-all satisfaction, and, conversely, those who increased activities tended to enjoy an increase in satisfaction. This finding is contrary to what might be predicted from disengagement theory which asserts that disengagement is associated with the maintenance of high morale (Cumming and Henry, 1961). Even though disengagement is more than reduced activity, and morale is not exactly equivalent to our measure of satisfaction, it is fair to say that disengagement theory would probably predict no association or a negative association between changes in activity and changes in attitudes. That is, when activities decrease, attitudes should remain high or even increase, rather than decline as in our study.

This positive correlation of activity with attitudes supports rather the activity theory of aging which has been stated as the "American formula for happiness in old age . . . keep active" (Havighurst and Albrecht, 1953). This theory is favored by most of the practical workers in the field of gerontology:

> They believe that people should maintain the activities and attitudes of middle age as long as possible and then find substitutes for the activities which they must give up—substitutes for work when they are forced to retire; substitutes for clubs and associations which they must give up; substitutes for friends and loved ones whom they lose by death (Havighurst, 1961).

It may well be that disengagement theory is applicable to some and the activity theory is applicable to others; that some find most satisfaction in disengaging and others find most satisfaction in remaining active. But apparently in our panel the activity theory was most applicable to most of the participants.

Among the specific activities related to attitudes, change in economic activities were the most closely related to changes in total attitudes. This is congruent with Kutner's (1956) finding that having a job is more closely associated with high morale than is keeping busy with recreational activities. However, because the economic activities sub-scale contains an item on the restrictions on activities resulting from lower income we cannot be sure at this point whether it is the change in job status or change in income or both that account for the association with attitudes.

Changes in health had almost no association with changes in total attitudes. This is surprising in view of the substantial associations between health and activity on the one hand and between activity and attitudes on the other. Perhaps this indicates that unless health changes activity, there is little effect on attitudes.

Persistence of life style. There is a clear tendency for aged people to persist with the same relative levels of activities and attitudes as they grow older. Most of the correlations of earlier scores with scores three years later were .57 or higher; half were over .70 (Table 4). This means that over half of the variance in later scores can be accounted for by the earlier scores in the majority of comparisons. Correlations between scores at Time 1 with scores at Time 4 (ten years later) were much lower because of the greater time lapse which made possible a greater number of events that could change the relative levels of activity and attitudes.

This persistence in scores over three-year periods, and even over the entire ten years, indicates both that the inventories are fairly reliable and that patterns of behavior and attitudes among the aged tend to be fairly stable over long periods of time. This also supports the results of a different type of persistence analysis (Maddox, 1966).

However, the correlations do not show consistent trends toward increasing persistence in the later intervals. The men's correlations actually decline somewhat in the third interval. Thus, the idea that the aged become increasingly rigid and "set in their ways" is not supported by this data.

Table 5. Standard deviations for activity and attitude scores at four points in time

Variables	Time 1	Time 2	Time 3	Time 4
Men				
Total activities S. D.	6.2	6.5	6.1	5.4
Total attitudes S. D.	4.9	5.3	5.3	5.7
Women				
Total activities S. D.	5.8	6.3	6.6	5.7
Total attitudes S. D.	5.5	5.5	5.5	5.8

Increasing homogeneity. The standard deviations show no consistent trend toward either increasing homogeneity or differentiation (Table 5). The women's standard deviations remained about the same while the men's decreased in activities but increased in attitudes. However, there was a generally consistent decrease in differences between the mean scores for men and women (Tables 1 and 2). There is practically no difference left between men and women in their total attitude scores by Time 3 and 4.

Thus, these data do not support the ideas that the aged become more differentiated in their behavior or attitudes (Havighurst, 1957) or that the "sexes become increasingly divergent with age" (Neugarten, 1964). On the contrary, the decrease in differences between men and women is consistent with Cameron's (1968) recent finding of converging interests between aged men and women.

SUMMARY

Changes in activities and attitudes over a ten-year period among 127 panelists in a longitudinal study of aging were assessed by use of the Chicago Inventory of Activity and Attitudes. There was no significant over-all decrease in activities or attitudes among men and only small over-all decreases among women. This was interpreted as evidence contrary to the findings of most cross-sectional surveys and the commonly held assumption that most people become less active as they age. It was suggested that normal aging persons tend to compensate for reductions in some activities or attitudes by increases in others, or to compensate reductions at one point in time with increases at other times. The greater decreases among women seem to indicate that at this stage in life aging causes more over-all changes among women than men.

Changes in activities were positively correlated with changes in attitudes so that reductions in activity were associated with decreases in satisfaction. This was interpreted as contrary to disengagement theory but supportive of activity theory: the "American formula for happiness in old age . . . keep active."

There was a strong tendency for the panelists to persist with the same over-all level of activities and attitudes over time, but there was no evidence that patterns of behavior or attitudes became increasingly rigid or differentiated. In fact, mean differences between men and women tended to disappear.

REFERENCES

Blalock, H. M.: Causal Inferences in Nonexperimental Research. Univ. N.C. Press, Chapel Hill, 1961

Burke, C. J.: Measurement scales and statistical models. In: M. H. Marx (Editor), Theories in Contemporary Psychology. Macmillan Co., New York, 1963.

Cavan, R. S., E. W. Burgess, R. J. Havighurst, and H. Goldhamer: Personal Adjustment in Old Age. Science Research Associates, Chicago, 1949, 204 pp.

Cameron, P.: Masculinity-feminity in the aged. J. Geront. **10**:63-65, 1968.

Cumming, E., and W. E. Henry: Growing Old. Basic Books, New York, 1961.

Goldfarb, N.: Longitudinal Statistical Analysis. Free Press, Glencoe, Ill., 1960.

Havighurst, R. J.: Validity of the Chicago Attitude Inventory as a measure of personal adjustment in old age. J. Abnorm. (Soc.) Psychol. **461**:24-29, 1951.

Havighurst, R. J.: The social competence of middle-aged people. Genet. Psychol. Monogr. **56**:297-375, 1957.

Havighurst, R. J.: Successful aging. Gerontologist **1**:4-7, 1961.

Havighurst, R. J., and R. Albrecht: Older People. Longmans, Green, New York, 1953.

Jeffers, F. C., and C. R. Nichols: The relationship of activities and attitudes to physical well-being in older people. J. Geront. **16**:67-70, 1961.

Kleemeier, R. W.: Leisure and disengagement in retirement. Gerontologist **4**:180-184, 1964.

Kutner, B.: Five hundred over sixty. Russell Sage Foundation, New York, 1956.

Labovitz, S.: Some observations on measurement and statistics. Soc. Forces **46**:151-160, 1967.

Maddox, G.: A longitudinal, multidisciplinary study of human aging. Proc. Social Statistics Section, Amer. Stat. Ass. 280-285, 1962.

Maddox, G.: Activity and morale: a longitudinal study of selected elderly subjects. Soc. Forces **42**:195-204, 1963.

Maddox, G.: Fact and artifact: evidence bearing on disengagement theory from the Duke Geriatrics Project. Hum. Develop. **8**:117-130, 1965.

Maddox, G.: Persistence of life style among the elderly. Proc. 7th Internat. Congr. Geront., Wien. Med. Akad., Wien, 1966.

Moberg, D. O.: Religiosity in old age, Gerontologist **51**:78-87, 1965.

Neugarten, B. L.: A developmental view of adult personality. In: J. E. Birren (Editor), Relations of Development and Aging. Charles C Thomas, Springfield, Ill., 1964.

HUMAN SEXUALITY AND THE HEALTHY ELDERLY

Nancy Fugate Woods, R.N., M.N.*

Within this culture there is a growing acceptance of sex as a natural function, provided that it is engaged in by consenting young adults. Such acceptance has not yet included the extremes of the life cycle, even though there is recognition that we are all sexual beings, beginning in utero. Sexuality during middle age and postretirement years has only recently received the attention of health science investigators; consequently myths about the sexual older years still abound.

This chapter will attempt to demonstrate that there is no single point in human existence at which sexual behavior reaches an obligatory halt. Instead, the biological changes that occur with the aging process and their impact on sexual behavior will be examined in the context of psychological variables such as interest, attitudes, and beliefs and the social variables such as stereotypes of aging, partner availability, and obstacles to sexual expression among the aging. Although an extensive literature exists dealing with the effects of various pathological conditions and pharmacological agents on sexual function, these topics will be only briefly mentioned here, since the focus is on healthy aging.

THE AGING PROCESS AND SEXUAL FUNCTION

The aging woman. Masters and Johnson (1966) described changes in sexual function in a population of sixty-one aging women, twenty-seven of whom were from 41 to 50 years and thirty-four of whom were from 51 to 78 years of age. Involutionary changes were noted in these women, involving breast tissue as well as genitalia. The steroid-starved vaginal walls of postmenopausal women appeared nearly as thin as tissue paper and no longer possessed the corrugated look

*Associate Professor of Nursing, Duke University, Durham, North Carolina.

Table 1. Phase-specific changes in the sexual response cycle of aging women*

Target tissue	Phase of sexual response			
	Excitement	Plateau	Orgasm	Resolution
Breast	Vasocongestive increase in size less pronounced, especially in more pendulous breasts	Engorgement of areola less intense	—	Loss of nipple erection slowed
Skin	Sex flush does not occur as frequently	Sex flush does not occur as frequently	—	—
Muscle	Degree of myotonia decreases with age	Degree of myotonia decreases with age	—	—
Urethra and urinary bladder	—	—	Minimal distention of meatus†	—
Rectum	—	—	Contraction of rectal sphincter only with severe tension levels	—
Clitoris	—	—	—	Retracts rapidly; tumescence lost rapidly

Labia majora	No women past age 51 demonstrated flattening, separation, and elevation of labia majora	—	—	—
Labia minora	Vasocongestion reduced	Labial color change (sex skin) usually pathognomonic of orgasm decreased in frequency among women 61 years of age and older	—	—
Bartholin's glands	—	Reduction in amount of secretions and activity, especially among postmenopausal women	—	—
Vagina	Rate and amount of vaginal lubrication decreased; lubrication occurs 1 to 3 minutes after stimulation; vaginal expansion in breadth and width decreases	Inner two thirds of vagina may still be expanding during this phase; vasocongestion of orgasmic platform reduced in intensity	Postmenopausal orgasmic platform contracts 3 to 5 times versus 5 to 10 times in younger women	Rapid involution and loss of vasocongestion
Cervix	—	—	—	Dilation of cervix not noted
Uterus	Uterine elevation and tenting of transcervical vagina develops more slowly and is less marked	Uterine elevation and tenting of transcervical vagina develops more slowly and is less marked	Some women report painful contractions with orgasm	—

*Summary of findings from The aging female. In Masters, William, and Johnson, Virginia. *Human sexual response.* Boston: Little, Brown & Co., 1966, pp. 223-247.
†Mechanical irritation of urethra and bladder may occur as a result of thinning of vagina, which minimizes protection of these structures during thrusting.

characteristic of the younger woman's vagina. Additionally, the color of the vaginal walls changed from a reddish purple associated with youth to a light pink color. Diminishing of the vaginal length and width were noted, as was a loss of elasticity of the vaginal wall. In addition, some atrophy of the breast tissue was noted.

Phase-specific changes seen among these aging women during the sexual response were also described and will be reviewed according to the progression of the sexual response cycle.

Excitement. During the excitement phase, the most notable changes involved vasocongestive phenomena. First, the rate of production and amount of vaginal lubrication diminished. Among the women 60 years of age and older, from 1 to 3 minutes were required for adequate lubrication. An interesting exception to this finding occurred among three women who were consistently sexually active, continuing to have intercourse once or twice weekly: they had no such interference with lubrication.* Changes in vasocongestive phenomena were also noted in other target organs: flattening, separation, and elevation of the labia majora disappeared among women past 50 years of age, and vasocongestion of the labia minora diminished. Vaginal expansion decreased in both breadth and width, uterine elevation and tenting developed more slowly and was less marked, and the degree of myotonia or muscle tension also appeared to decrease with age.

Plateau. During the plateau phase, further changes linked to a diminished vasocongestive capacity were evident: areolar engorgement of the breast appeared less intense, labial color change was observed less frequently among women past 60 years of age, and the swelling of the orgasmic platform appeared reduced in intensity. Additionally, the secretions from Bartholin's glands had diminished among the postmenopausal women.

Orgasm. With orgasm, there were fewer contractions of the orgasmic platform than seen in premenopausal women, and some women reported discomfort caused by uterine contractions. In addition, minimal distention of the urinary meatus was observed, and contraction of the rectal sphincter occurred only with severe levels of sexual tension.

Resolution. During the resolution phase, nipple erection occurred more slowly than among younger women, but the clitoris retracted from underneath the hood rapidly, and tumescence of both the clitoris and the orgasmic platform subsided quickly.

Summary. These changes are summarized in Table 1. It should be noted that sexual response in the aging woman is as similar to that of the younger woman as it is dissimilar. The changes just described are primarily caused by steroid starvation accompanying the menopause and do not make cessation of sexual activity an imperative. As the woman ages, the duration and intensity of the phys-

---

*This phenomenon may be analogous in some respects to disuse atrophy, a wasting of tissue seen in immobilized limbs.

iological responses to sexual stimulation do diminish gradually. However, each of the phases of the sexual response cycle can be observed, and orgasmic experience is not precluded by the aging process. Satisfying sexual function can persist far into later life, providing the woman is in reasonably good health and has an interested and interesting partner (Masters and Johnson, 1966).

The aging man. Masters and Johnson (1966) also described sexual function among thirty-nine aging men, ranging from 51 to 89 years of age. In general, they found that as men age, physiological changes in sexual response parallel those seen in women. The increased duration of each phase of the sexual response cycle was the most characteristic change seen with increasing age. The ways in which sexual response of aging men differs from that of their younger counterparts are summarized in Table 2.

Excitement and plateau. During the excitement phase vasocongestive changes occurred more slowly or appeared to be much less intense than among younger males. Erection happened more slowly and could be maintained for extended periods of time without ejaculation. If the man's erection was lost, a secondary refractory period may have occurred, that is, a period of time during which another erection could not be attained despite the quality or intensity of stimulation. There was also decreased evidence of vasocongestion in the scrotal sac, and the scrotum appeared less tense than in younger men. The testes of aging men did not elevate fully to the perineum, and rarely was a vasocongestive increase in testicular size observed. Additionally, nipple erection became less discernible, and the sex flush did not occur as frequently. As with aging women, the degree of myotonia decreased. During the plateau phase, the only other remarkable difference between older and younger men appeared to be the lack of color change at the coronal ridge of the penis.

Orgasm. With orgasm, there were fewer contractions of the penis and rectal sphincter. In addition, the force of ejaculation was decreased among these aging men. It was posited that this reduced force of expulsion may have contributed to the older man's not perceiving the stage of ejaculatory inevitability as his younger counterparts did. In some instances, especially if the aging man had maintained his erection for a long period of time, seepage of semen took the place of a more forceful ejaculation; these men did not associate psychosexual satisfaction with seepage of semen.

Resolution. In general, the resolution period occurred more rapidly in aging men. The erection was quickly lost, and testicular descent occurred shortly after ejaculation. Only vasocongestion of the scrotum and nipple erection disappeared slowly. Usually the refractory period lengthened with the man's age. Although many of these changes could be anxiety provoking, Masters and Johnson point out that the aging man actually has the advantage of improved ejaculatory control, and he simultaneously experiences a reduced ejaculatory demand. This means that he may be satisfied to ejaculate during every second or third intercourse, rather than with each attempt. These investigators appear optimistic

Table 2. Phase-specific changes in the sexual response cycle of aging men*

Target tissue	Phase of sexual response			
	Excitement	Plateau	Orgasm	Resolution
Breast	Nipple erection less discernible	—	—	Nipple erection lost more slowly
Skin	Sex flush does not occur as frequently	Sex flush does not occur as frequently	—	—
Muscle	Degree of myotonia decreased	Degree of myotonia decreased	—	—
Rectum	—	—	Rectal sphincter contractions decreased in frequency	—
Penis	Erection may be less full; erection requires two or three times as much time as necessary for younger males; erection can be maintained for extended periods without ejaculation; if erection is lost without ejaculation, there may be a secondary refractory period (rare in men under 50 years)	Color change at coronal ridge not observed in men over 60 years of age	Ejaculatory force is decreased (expulsion of semen 6 to 12 inches versus 12 to 14 inches in younger men); volume of semen decreases; fewer contractions with orgasm	Refractory period lasts for extended period; rapid loss of erection
Scrotum	Decreased evidence of vasocongestion; less tensing of scrotal sac evident	—	—	Slow involution of vasocongestion
Testes	Testes do not elevate fully to perineum; less contractile tone of cremasteric musculature observed; rare vasocongestive increase in size	—	—	Testicular descent extremely rapid

*Summary of findings from The aging male. In Masters, William, and Johnson, Virginia. *Human sexual response.* Boston: Little, Brown & Co., 1966, pp. 248-270.

about the aging man's ability to still enjoy a full and satisfying sexual relationship provided that he is in relatively good health and has an interested and interesting partner.

Nocturnal erections. Appreciation of sex as a natural function has recently led researchers to investigate the occurrence of penile erections during sleep. Early reports of research conducted using male subjects in their twenties and thirties revealed that either full or partial erection occurred in 95% of the rapid eye movement (REM) periods, and the erections appeared to be synchronous with these dream periods (Fischer and associates, 1965). Later investigations confirmed the occurrence of erections associated with the REM period of the sleep cycle among men between 71 and 96 years of age (Kahn and Fisher, 1969a and b). Although the percentage of REM periods accompanied by erection was smaller than that observed for younger men, 45% of these periods were accompanied by a full or moderate erection. An interesting incidental finding of this study was the highly sexual content associated with those dreams which the subjects were able to recall. When recounting these dreams, the subjects often indicated their discomfort, since the dream material "was improper" (Kahn and Fisher, 1969b). A more recent investigation of REM sleep and nocturnal erections in aging men ranging from 60 to 69 years of age revealed that cyclical occurrence of erections persisted but in some instances during the non-REM portion of the sleep cycle (Karacan and associates, 1972).

These data, coupled with the findings of Masters and Johnson, indicate that although the nature of male sexual response changes with the aging process, men in unimpaired health most likely possess the ability to attain erections. Even in instances in which a partner is not available, sexuality persists in the content of dreams and on a cyclic basis during sleep.

PREVALENCE AND INCIDENCE OF SEXUAL BEHAVIOR AMONG AGING PERSONS

Having addressed the physiological changes that occur with the aging process, I shall examine the prevalence of various types of sexual behavior among aging persons, the reported incidence of sexual behavior, and the factors that may influence the frequency with which aging persons are sexually active. An attempt has been made to summarize the findings of this large body of literature in Table 3. The reader will note difficulty in making comparisons between the studies because investigators studied different variables and did not use uniform definitions or summary statistics in all instances. In general, findings are available regarding both intercourse and masturbation; changes in other forms of sexual behavior will be described when appropriate data are available. A review of this literature will be followed by a summary of the general trends reflected in Table 3.

The Kinsey studies. Early studies in the area of sexual behavior were conducted by Kinsey and his associates, and, although elderly persons comprised

Table 3. Incidence and frequencies of sexual behaviors among research populations of well aging persons

Study	Population	Prevalence of sexual behavior		Comments
		Intercourse	Masturbation	

Kinsey and associates (1948)

Population: 126 men, 87 white, 39 black, 60 yr and older

Intercourse — Mean frequency per week:

Age	Mean frequency per week
65	1.0
75	0.3
80	0.1

(N for each group not given)

Masturbation: Presence documented in histories of some men in 71- to 86-year-old age range

Comments: Frequency of intercourse was noted for white men only. 20% of men impotent age 60 and 75% at age 80

Kinsey and associates (1953)

Population: 431 women ranging from 46 to 60 years of age

Intercourse — Mean frequency per week:

Age	Mean frequency per week	N
46 to 50	1.4	261
51 to 55	1.2	120
56 to 60	0.8	50

Masturbation: In 46- to 60-year span, frequency decreased among married and previously married women with age but remained nearly constant among single women with a mean frequency of about 1.0 per week

Comments: Frequency of intercourse restricted to marital coitus

Christenson and Gagnon (1965)

Population: 241 white women 50 years and older from case history files of Institute for Sex Research; data are for marital sexual activities

	Intercourse		Masturbation	Data for sex dreams
Age	Median frequency per year	N	Median frequency per year	Median frequency per year
50	69.4	160	13.3	3.1
55	57.9	74	3.7	3.0
60	40.7	33	—	—
65	—	16	—	—
70	—	3	—	—

	Intercourse			Masturbation		Dreams to orgasm	
Age	Incidence (%)	N	Age	Incidence (%)	Age	Incidence (%)
50	87.5	160	50	31.2	50	27.0
55	89.2	74	55	29.7	55	26.0
60	69.7	33	60	27.3	60	18.2
65	50.0	16	65	25.0	65	18.8
70	—	3	70	—	70	—

Christenson and Johnson (1973) 71 never-married white women aged 50 years and over from case history files of Institute for Sex Research

Intercourse			Masturbation		Dreams to orgasm	
Age	Incidence (%)	N	Age	Incidence (%)	Age	Incidence (%)
45	32	71	45	49	45	18
50	25	71	50	44	50	20
55	15	34	55	35	55	6
60	8	14	60	23	60	0

71 women followed retrospectively by history

Finkle and associates (1959) 101 randomly selected clinic patients, excluding genito-urinary problems

Intercourse			Percent sexually active
Age	Frequency per year	N	
55 to 59	29	16	69
60 to 64	28	16	63
65 to 69	12	19	63
70 to 74	25	28	39
75 to 79	11	17	24
80+	5	10	40

Frequency per year represents average age for age band

Continued.

Table 3. Incidence and frequencies of sexual behaviors among research populations of well aging persons—cont'd

Study	Population	Prevalence of sexual behavior		Comments
		Intercourse	**Masturbation**	
Freeman (1961)	74 male respondents; population sampled included physician's patients, etc.; initial number to whom questionnaire was sent not known	Frequency of intercourse decreased with age **Persistence of ability** Number Percent 41 55.4% **Persistence of desire** Number Percent 56 75.6%		Absence of spouse or illness influenced sexual activity
Rubin (1965)	Questionnaire survey of aging men sent to 6000 men 65 and older listed in Who's Who in America; 832 replies	60% indicated satisfactory coitus; 30% were impotent; incidence of satisfactory coitus decreased with age	25% indicated they masturbated	
Newman and Nichols (1960)	250 volunteer well aging persons	*Age band* *N* *Percent sexually active* 60 to 64 35 60 65 to 69 46 64 70 to 74 41 58 75+ 27 26		These data represent findings on 149 married couples; men exceeded women in mean percent still sexually active

Intercourse

Pfeiffer and associates (1969) | 39 survivors of cohort of 254 for whom data on sexual interest and activity were complete for all four studies (exams conducted at 3-year intervals) | Marital sexual activity in both men and women tended to decrease over time; sexual activity and interest actually increased for some | Proportion of men continuing to demonstrate sexual interest over 10-year period exceeded that for women; study is significant in that it is limited to biologically advantaged aging and permits examination of longitudinal data on sexual interest and activity

Pfeiffer and associates (1972) | 502 well aging persons 45 to 69 years of age (261 white men and 241 white women) | *(see tables below)* | Awareness of a decline in interest and activity occurred between 46 and 50 years of age; primary reason for stopping intercourse attributed to men by both spouses

Data for women

Frequency of intercourse (%)

Age	N	None	Month-ly	Once a wk +
46 to 50	43	14	26	60
51 to 55	41	20	41	39
56 to 60	48	42	27	31
61 to 65	44	61	29	10
66 to 71	55	73	16	11
Total	231	44	27	28

Data for men

Frequency of intercourse (%)

Age	N	None	Month-ly	Once a wk +
46 to 50	43	0	5	95
51 to 55	41	5	29	66
56 to 60	61	7	38	55
61 to 65	54	20	43	37
66 to 71	62	24	48	28
Total	261	12	34	54

only a small portion of this study population, these data are worthy of examination. Kinsey and associates (1948) interviewed 126 men, 60 years of age and older, eighty-seven of whom were white. For the white men in this sample, the mean frequency of intercourse per week decreased with age. Although data are not available regarding changes in masturbatory behavior with age, there was documentation of masturbation in the histories of some of the men in the 71- to 86-year-old age range. Furthermore, Kinsey noted that the percent of men in this group who were impotent tend to increase with age. Whereas 20% of the men were impotent at age 60, 75% reported impotence at age 80.

In the volume devoted to sexual behavior of women, Kinsey and associates (1953) present data regarding the sexual behavior of 431 women ranging from 46 to 60 years of age. The mean frequency of intercourse per week decreased over each age band. Masturbatory frequency also decreased with age among the married and previously married women but remained nearly constant among single women throughout this age range. Unfortunately, similar data were not discussed with regard to those women over 60 years of age because of their small numbers.

Studies of aging women. Christenson and Gagnon (1965) explored the histories of 241 white women who were 50 years of age or older at the time they were interviewed by the Institute for Sex Research. Never-married women were selected from the files to ensure some uniformity of their social experiences. Data are reported for women ranging in age from 50 to 70. An aging effect on sexual behavior was observed among this group of women, differing with type of sexual activity; marital status apparently influenced their patterns of behavior. For the married women, incidence of coitus appeared to decrease with age, as did masturbatory behavior and experiencing sexual dreams to orgasm. It is interesting to note that the decrease in frequency of the latter two behaviors was less pronounced than that experienced with regard to intercourse. Among the postmarital women, there existed considerably different patterns of behavior. Even though these women lacked a legally sanctioned partner, 37% of those who were 50 still reported they were having intercourse. This figure dropped to about 12% in the 60-year age group and disappeared entirely from the later age bands. Incidence of masturbation was nearly double that for the married women, with 59% of the women reporting that they masturbated at age 50 and 25% of the women at age 70. It is also interesting to note that sexual dreams leading to orgasm never entirely disappeared, even among the women who were 70.

Christenson and Gagnon also reported that the sexual activity levels of women before age 30 did not seem to be related to marital sexual activity after age 50 but did seem to be positively associated with postmarital coitus. Although education did not seem to influence the women's sexual behavior patterns in later life, religious devoutness as determined by church attendance did, in a negative direction. Finally, women in this sample with younger spouses tended to have higher coital rates than those with older spouses.

Christenson and Johnson (1973) examined data similar to that reported above in relation to seventy-one never-married white women. About 33% of this sample reported they had never experienced intercourse. The incidence of women having intercourse, masturbating, and experiencing dreams to orgasms decreased with age. A dropoff in all three activities was evident by age 55. Generally, those women who had a high level of activity in early life were those who were active well into later life. Indeed, some of the women reported being multiply orgasmic into their fifties and sixties. Eight of the women with homosexual backgrounds demonstrated an aging pattern similar to the sexually active women in the rest of the sample. Menopause was associated with no change in erotic levels for half of the women and with an equally frequent increase and decrease among the remaining women.

Studies of aging men. Finkle and associates (1959) interviewed 101 randomly selected clinic patients, excluding any with genitourinary problems from the sample. These men ranged in age from 55 to 86 years of age. For the purposes of this study, potency was defined as the ability to copulate at least once within the past year. There was a general decline in the ability to have intercourse, with 65% of the men under 70 retaining their potency as opposed to 34% of those over 70. The percentage of men sexually active decreased with age, as did the frequency of intercourse. This study also determined that men gave several reasons (in addition to impotence) for discontinuing intercourse, including no desire for sexual activity, absence of a partner, and refusal of the partner.

Freeman (1961) distributed a questionnaire to an unspecified number of men, receiving returns from seventy-four of these. The population sampled for this study included physicians' private practices, organizations, recommendations by volunteers, and persons named by physicians and social workers. The average age of the sample was 71 with a range from 64 to 91 years. What is notable about Freeman's results is that the aging male's desire for sexual activity exceeded the persistence of his ability as he aged.

Rubin (1965) also reports data about the sexual activity of aging males. He distributed questionnaires to 6000 men listed in *Who's Who in America* who were over the age of 65; 832 replies were received. Seventy percent of the married respondents engaged in intercourse on a regular basis. Among the group of 104 men aged 75 to 92, almost half reported intercourse was still satisfactory. Of this group, 30% indicated that they were impotent, but a majority of the total sample reported they still had morning erections. About 25% of the entire group currently were masturbating or had done so after they were 60.

The Duke studies. The most extensive survey research done in the area of sexuality and healthy aging has been conducted by investigators from the Duke Center for the Study of Aging and Human Development. Since 1953, a continuous study involving aging subjects residing in the central portion of North Carolina has been conducted by an inter-disciplinary team. Each subject has been studied intensively, some having as many as two 8-hour periods of testing during each study period. None of these subjects is a resident of a nursing home or hospital, and as a group they represent a generally successful adaptation to aging. Although the overall study design incorporates a longitudinal approach to data collection, some of the data discussed here will result from cross-sectional analyses. Therefore, when the results pertain to longitudinal findings, this will be specified.

In 1960 Newman and Nichols reported results of an investigation of the sexual activities and attitudes in 250 persons between the ages of 60 and 93. These subjects included women as well as men, blacks and whites, and married and nonmarried persons. Of the 149 persons who were still married and living with their spouses, 54% indicated they were sexually active in contrast to 7% of the nonmarried. A significantly lower level of sexual activity appeared among participants 75 years of age and older. This was often attributable to loss of the spouse or to debilitating illnesses. Women in the sample reported less sexual activity than men, whites less than blacks, and those of high socioeconomic status less than those of low socioeconomic status. Every participant rated strength of sexual drives as lower in their old age than in earlier life. However, there was a trend for strength of sexual interest to persist throughout the life cycle: those who had relatively strong sexual urges in youth were more likely than those with less strong urges to maintain moderate levels of sexual feelings in old age.

Pfeiffer and associates (1968) reported results of a longitudinal investigation that included data obtained at 3- to 4-year intervals. The number of subjects was 254 for the first data collection period but was subsequently reduced to 190 and 126, respectively, during the last two periods. At the first interview the average age of the subjects was 70.93. Intraindividual changes in sexual activity were observed over two interviews for 160 subjects and revealed a variety of patterns: the most prevalent pattern for subjects for whom data were available was not to be sexually active at either occasion. However, 30% of these subjects indicated that their sexual activity had remained the same as or had increased from the time of the first interview. This finding is in contrast to the cross-sectional data for the entire sample, which indicated a decline in sexual activity with aging. Intraindividual changes in sexual interest were also observed for 116 subjects. It is interesting to note that 14% of the subjects reported rising patterns of sexual interest.*

Subjects who had discontinued sexual intercourse prior to completion of the entire study were asked to indicate the factors responsible. Death of the spouse was the most common reason, followed by illness of a spouse, loss of potency, and finally loss of interest. When death of the spouse was eliminated, it appeared

---

*A third finding of great importance was the presence of congruence of reporting between spouse pairs. Among the thirty-one spouse pairs in the larger sample, there was 91% agreement in the reporting of sexual data.

that in most instances the husbands and wives both attributed cessation of inter-course to the male. Data were also available with regard to the age at which inter-course was discontinued. For men and women, respectively, the median ages were 68 and 60 (Pfeiffer and associates, 1968).

A later report by these same investigators focused on thirty-nine subjects who had survived throughout all four data collection periods. These persons were regarded as biologically advantaged individuals, so these results reflect the sexual behavior patterns that can be generalized to elderly who are in optimum health (Pfeiffer and associates, 1969). The average age of these subjects was 67.23 at the first interview and 76.89 at the last. The proportion of men who con-tinued to be interested in sex remained high during the entire 10-year period. However, this was not the case for women: a lower proportion of women demon-strated continuing sexual interest. Both the men and women experienced a de-cline in sexual activity over time, but the activity for women was lower than that for men throughout the studies. The investigators note that the interest-activity gap seen in men increased in magnitude as they aged, but this was not evident among women. In fact, interest and activity for these women remained low throughout the study.

The Duke program later explored sexual interest and activity during the middle years (Pfeiffer and associates, 1972). Two hundred and sixty-one men and 241 women between the ages of 46 and 69 years from middle and upper socioeconomic levels were interviewed regarding their sexual behavior. Men from each age group generally reported greater sexual interest and activity than women from corresponding age ranges. A decline in overall interest and activity was again seen in this age range. There was strong evidence that sex continued to be an important aspect of middle life. Only 6% of the men and 33% of the women in the sample no longer expressed an interest in sex, and only 12% of the women were no longer sexually active. These persons reported a notice-able decline in sexual interest and activity during the ages of 46 to 50 and 51 to 55 years. As in the earlier study, women attributed cessation of sexual relations to their husbands, the husbands concurring.

A later study of these same subjects (Pfeiffer and Davis, 1972) indicated that the level of sexual functioning in younger years, age, present health status, social class, antihypertensive drug therapy, present life satisfaction, physical function rating, and excess worry over physical examination findings all influenced the level of current sexual functioning among the middle-aged men. For women, marital status and age were the most significant determinants in addition to past sexual enjoyment. Thus those who had enjoyed sex during their youth were more likely to continue to do so during middle age. For women, presence of a capable and socially acceptable partner seemed to be a more significant variable. This may also explain why the woman's age is a determinant of her behavior, since it is likely that her spouse's age would be correlated with hers and probably re-lated to his potency. In fact, these investigators suggest that the middle-aged woman may adaptively inhibit her sexual interests in the absence of an acceptable partner. For men, age contributed negatively as expected. Use of drugs likely to induce impotence and indices of physical and psychosocial well-being both influenced sexual activity in the expected direction.

A note on the aging homosexual. Weinberg and Williams (1974) surveyed 3667 persons from various locations in the United States, receiving 1057 returns from male homosexuals. (Homosexuals from the Netherlands and Denmark were also included in the study). These investigators found that older homosexuals were less involved in the homosexual world, had homosexual sex less frequently, and were more likely to be living alone than their younger counterparts. In contrast to popular beliefs, the older homosexuals were no worse off on selected measures of psychological dimensions than the younger homosexuals, and in some instances they were better off. The investigators concluded that the stereotype that portrays the homosexual declining in psychological health as he ages probably results from overgeneralizing meanings to the social and sexual situations of the older homosexual that he in actuality does not experience.

Summary. Definite trends are evident in the previously cited literature. First, there does not seem to be a single point in the life cycle at which sexual activity for either sex must cease. There is, however, a decline in both reported sexual interest and activity with the aging process. As men age, the proportion able to engage in intercourse decreases. Marital status seemed to be a more significant determinant of sexual behavior for women than for men. It was suggested that aging women adaptively inhibit their sexual interest in the absence of a partner who is socially acceptable and/or physically capable of intercourse. Level of sexual interest during youth influenced the person's expressed interest during the middle and late years.

PSYCHOSOCIAL VARIABLES INFLUENCING SEXUALITY OF THE HEALTHY AGING

The taboo against sex in old age is alive and well. According to Pfeiffer (1969), its origins probably lie in the assumption that sex is primarily for procreation, not recreation. Once the possibility or desirability of reproduction is no longer an issue, the assumption is made that sex is therefore no longer appropriate. It is also possible that this taboo is an extension of the incest taboo. The anxiety engendered among children about their parents' involvement in sexual activity may spill over into adulthood, thus discouraging sexual expression among the aged. Finally, Pfeiffer notes that the younger generation can eliminate the elderly from competition for sexual objects by portraying them as an asexual group.

Whatever the origins of the taboo against sexuality for the aging, it has made a significant impact on the beliefs of not only aging persons themselves but also on members of the health professions, researchers, and society in general. What may be interpreted as interest in a young man becomes lechery in an older man; similar aspersions are cast in the direction of aging women.

Aging women. In addition to the taboo just described, the aging face a number of other psychosocial obstacles to functioning sexually. As we discussed earlier, aging women frequently face the problem of no partner or a partner no longer able to function sexually. Lacking opportunity, the woman's sexual interest may adaptively diminish.

Next, psychological upsets associated with menopause have been cited as potential interferences with sexual functioning in aging women (Masters and Johnson, 1966). They add that women who receive little satisfaction from their sexual relationships or actually find them repugnant may use their age as a culturally acceptable way to relieve themselves from their so-called marital duty. Finally, Masters and Johnson found that some of their interview sample of 152 women 51 years of age and older actually believed that intercourse was unsuitable for the aged, and therefore they were no longer sexually active.

Neugarten and associates (1963) concluded that younger women held more negative and undifferentiated attitudes on the basis of questionnaires about menopause administered to 100 healthy women ranging in age from 21 to 65 years. The youngest women disagreed most with the view that menopausal women could experience an increase in sexual interest or drive. The women in the 45- to 55-year age range expressed a wide variety of views ranging from a decreased interest in sex, since procreation was no longer possible, to an upsurge, since fear of pregnancy was removed. Some of these views were probably related to the middle-aged woman's life experiences.

Maoz and associates (1970) were unable to demonstrate a relationship between coping with earlier psychosexual phenomena and attitudes toward menopause among their sample of fifty-five women, eleven of whom were psychiatric patients. In general, the women's attitudes were more likely to be mixed than totally positive or negative. Interestingly enough, reported dissatisfaction with sex was associated with a negative view of menopause. Slight differences were noted among women of various ethnic groups.

Aging men. The belief that sex for the aging person is not socially acceptable was also found among aging men in the sample of 212 men 51 years of age and older interviewed by Masters and Johnson (1966). Additionally, cessation of sexual intercourse was sometimes associated with monotony in the relationship, usually because of boredom with the partner. Some men attributed their inactivity to preoccupation with their careers or financial affairs. Others blamed either physical or psychological fatigue. Another factor mentioned as responsible for inability to function sexually was overindulgence in either food or drink. Physical or emotional problems of the man or his spouse were also cited frequently. Finally, fear of failure lurked in the minds of several men. Having failed once at intercourse, these men often withdrew from their regular sexual activity rather than risk embarrassment on another occasion.

Studies of thirty aging couples indicate that although sexual potency does not appear to differentiate the happily married from the less happy, frequency of sexual relations was greater among the happier group (Busse and Eisdorfer, 1970). These results suggest that sexual activity may remain an important component of marital happiness throughout the aging process.

Is sexuality among the aging changing? Morton Hunt's (1974) data on sexual behavior in the 1970s indicated a slight change in sexual behavior among aging persons. Hunt surveyed 2026 persons in twenty-four cities in the United States. Comparing his data to that of Kinsey's, Hunt concluded that there has been a slight increase in the frequency of reported marital coitus among those between 46 and 60 years of age. Unfortunately, no data are presented dealing with persons older than 60. Hunt inferred that sex is becoming more suitable and less disgraceful for the middle-aged in our society. He also attributes the increase in frequency of marital coitus to the availability of hormonal therapy for menopausal women, which decreases discomfort during intercourse caused by steroid starvation. Finally, Hunt indicates that the increase in variety of coital techniques used may be keeping marital coitus interesting for longer periods of time.

CONCLUSION

It is hoped that the atmosphere of tolerance for sexual expression will encompass the aging during the next few generations, that the final item of the

---

BILL OF RIGHTS TO GUARANTEE
SEXUAL FREEDOM*

The right to express yourself as a sexual being

The right to be self-confident and self-directing in regard to your sexuality

The right to become the person you would like to be

The right to select and be with a sex partner of your choice, whether it be of the same sex or of the opposite sex

The right to be aware of the influence your sexuality can have on someone else and to use it in a constructive and therapeutic manner

The right to encourage your peer group members to function as sexual beings

The right to assist others in asserting and expressing their sexuality

The right to be accepting and tolerant of another's sexual attitudes and preferences

The right to assist men and women of all ages to recognize their sexuality as an integral part of their personality, inherited at conception, molded and tempered by environment, sustained by health, threatened by disease, and reversed by choice

---

*From Jacobson, Linbania. Illness and human sexuality. *Nursing Outlook,* 1974, **22**(1), 50-53.

Bill of Rights to Guarantee Sexual Freedom (p. 86) will not be last in priority, and that aging persons who are in good health will be comfortable expressing their sexuality. After all, sex is a part of being human and an important aspect of being alive.

REFERENCES

Busse, Ewald, and Eisdorfer, Carl. Two thousand years of married life. In Palmore, Erdman (Ed.). *Normal aging: reports from the Duke Longitudinal Study, 1955-1969.* Durham, N.C.: Duke University Press, 1970.

Christenson, C. V., and Gagnon, J. H. Sexual behavior in a group of older women. *Journal of Gerontology,* 1965, **20,** 351-356.

Christenson, C. V., and Johnson, A. B. Sexual patterns in a group of older never-married women. *Journal of Geriatric Psychiatry,* 1973, **7**(1), 88-98.

Finkle, A., Moyers, T., Tobenkin, M., and Karg, S. Sexual potency in aging males: frequency of coitus among clinic patients. *Journal of the American Medical Association,* 1959, 170, 1391-1393.

Fischer, C., and associates. Cycle of penile erection synchronous with dreaming (REM) sleep. Preliminary report. *Archives of General Psychiatry,* 1965, **12,** 29-45.

Freeman, J. Sexual capacities in the aging male. *Geriatrics,* January, 1961, **16,** 37-43.

Hunt, M. *Sexual behavior in the seventies.* Chicago: Playboy Press, 1974.

Jacobson, L. Illness and human sexuality. *Nursing Outlook,* 1974, **22**(1), 50-53.

Kahn, E., and Fisher, C. REM sleep and sexuality in the aged. *Journal of Geriatric Psychiatry,* 1969a, **2,** 181-199.

Kahn, E., and Fisher, C. Some correlates of rapid eye movement sleep in the normal aged male. *Journal of Nervous and Mental Diseases,* 1969b, **148,** 495-505.

Karacan, I., Hursch, C. J., and Williams, R. L. Some characteristics of nocturnal penile tumescence in elderly males, *Journal of Gerontology* 1972, **27,** 39-45.

Kinsey, A., Pomeroy, W., and Martin, C. *Sexual behavior in the human male.* Philadelphia: W. B. Saunders Co., 1948.

Kinsey, A., Pomeroy, W., Martin, C., and Gebhard, P. *Sexual behavior in the human female.* Philadelphia: W. B. Saunders Co., 1953.

Maoz, B., Dowty, N., Antonovsky, A., and Wijsenbeek, H. Female attitudes to menopause. *Social Psychiatry,* 1970, **5,** 35-40.

Masters, W., and Johnson, V. *Human sexual response.* Boston: Little, Brown & Co., 1966.

Neugarten, B., Wood, V., Kraines, R., and Loomis, B. Women's attitudes toward the menopause. *Vita Humana,* 1963, **6,** 140-151.

Newman, G., and Nichols, C. R. Sexual activities and attitudes in older persons. *Journal of the American Medical Association,* 1960, **173,** 33-35.

Pfeiffer, E. Sexual behavior in old age. In Busse, E. W., and Pfeiffer, E. (Eds.). *Behavior and adaption in late life.* Boston: Little, Brown & Co., 1969.

Pfeiffer, E., and Davis, G. C. Determinants of sexual behavior in middle and old age. *Journal of the American Geriatrics Society,* 1972, **20,** 151-158.

Pfeiffer, E., Verwoerdt, A., and Davis, G. C. Sexual behavior in middle life. *American Journal of Psychiatry,* 1972, **128,** 1262-1267.

Pfeiffer, E., Verwoerdt, A., and Wang, H. S. Sexual behavior in aged men and women: 1. Observation on 254 community volunteers. *Archives of General Psychiatry,* 1968, **19,** 753-758.

Pfeiffer, E., Verwoerdt, A., and Wang, H. S. The natural history of sexual behavior in a biologically advantaged group of aged individuals. *Journal of Gerontology,* 1969, **24,** 193-198.

Rubin, I. *Sexual life after sixty.* New York: Basic Books, 1965.

Weinberg, M., and Williams, C. *Male homosexuals: their problems and adaptations.* New York: Oxford University Press, 1974.

EATING AND AGING

Lillian E. Troll, Ph.D.*

In part, this paper is concerned with a dilemma underlying nutritional policy for the aged. The following paragraphs contain one set of statements that point in one direction matching with another set of statements that point in an opposite direction. Consider the first set of propositions:

(a) Eating is one of the most basic ways of living.

(b) The fact of their survival attests to the essential adequacy of the eating practices of old people. And more and more people are living into old age; at present, one out of ten people in the United States are over sixty-five.[1]

(c) Life in old age is much more a continuation of past ways of living than of marked change. The best prediction of what a person will be like when he gets old is that he will be like what he is now, and what he has been up to now, only more so. People seem to get more like themselves as they get older and less like other people. Variance of any characteristic increases, so that there is no such thing as an aged type of person.[2]

All of this suggests that it would be a mistake to adopt any fixed set of rules about diet and eating practices for older people and expect them to be good for *all* old people. In fact, other things being equal—if they ever are—the best eating practices for most older people are probably what they are already practicing. At any rate, it would not be wise for a professional nutritionist to institute any changes in an older person's eating practices before making sure that, first, there is something very wrong with those practices and, second, that the proposed changes are indeed an improvement. (Of course, this rule would apply to all the helping professions, not only those which are involved with nutrition.)

Reproduced from *Journal of the American Dietetic Association*, November, 1971, **59**, 456-459.
*Wayne State University, Detroit, Michigan.

THE OTHER SIDE OF THE COIN

Now consider this other set of statements:

(a) Good food is essential to good health

(b) The aging body becomes increasingly sensitive and less tolerant; food habits that could once have just produced minor discomforts, or no trouble at all, can cause serious illness in old age. Or, food that once caused pleasure can lead to discomfort.[3]

(c) Aging is usually accompanied by significant activity changes. In fact, one thing we can say for sure about ability and performance changes in the process of aging is that they are all in the direction of slowing down.[4] As we age, we become more sluggish and sedentary, and the food habits we acquired when we were younger, in a time of more abundant exercise and bodily movement, are no longer appropriate to our way of life.

(d) If food has been used as a comforter, there are more and more losses for which comfort is needed, and more and more desire for food the nourishment from which could well be dispensed with. The cost of survival is the outliving of many of the things that made life worth living. Those who live the longest necessarily experience the loss of most of the people they love, of most of their social involvements, and of most of the landmarks of existence that tell them who they are and where they have come from.

(e) Food costs money. Few old people in this country today raise their own food; they must buy it. Yet almost one-fourth of older Americans (over sixty-five) are poor and nearly all feel a squeeze on their fixed incomes.[5] Howell and Loeb state[3]: "A significant proportion of adults over the age of 65 in the United States do not have incomes adequate to purchase . . . a diet which provides for health and well-being" (p. 7). While not all old people are poor (and some are very rich indeed), for those who are poor, the buying of food either on the basis of past habits or on the basis of present optimal nutrition may be impossible. Something must be dropped. When a meat and potatoes and fruit family drops the meat and the fruit and keeps the potatoes because they are cheaper, there has been tremendous qualitative deterioration in their diet as a whole. A good diet is a *gestalt*, a whole combination of foods. If some foods are dropped for reasons of economy, the good effect is gone.

(f) Economy is not the only reason for dropping part of a diet. Lack of energy for shopping and for preparing certain foods is another important contributor to subtle but consequential changes in a diet *gestalt*. Whether this lessened energy comes from loss of vigor, from depression, or even in a circular way from loss of previous good eating habits, it leads to distortion of the nutritional pattern.

There is thus a primary contradiction between what in all probability is a proven good way of eating—proven by the fact of survival—and the physical and social changes that might make some of the past good ways no longer so good.

Two broad issues involved in evaluating the eating of the aging are the social nature of eating on one hand and the isolating consequences of aging on the other.

THE PROCESS OF AGING

Let us consider the general process of aging. Just as there is wide variation among individuals in time and speed of development, both toward early maturity and on into the later phases of the life cycle, so there is wide variation in time and speed of development and aging within any individual among bodily systems and social and psychologic processes. Vision, for example, starts aging at birth. But most biologic processes, such as strength, quick thinking, sexual power, or general vigor, increase from birth through childhood and adolescence to a high point in the twenties, followed by an apparent plateau through the years of maturity and middle age to a relatively slow decline thereafter. Other abilities, e.g., athletic, start to decline almost from the time of greatest power, in the middle twenties, and this decline usually proceeds rapidly. Still other abilities show no noticeable decrease until the very end of life; they may even exhibit a steady continuous increase. This is the case for the accumulation of information and vocabulary.[6,7]

Over the years, intelligence tests of populations of all ages have shown a steady increase in intelligence (I.Q.) to some time in the teens or the twenties with a steady decrease thereafter.[4,7] This has been widely interpreted as indicating that people lose their intellectual capacity from about the age of twenty—a most depressing thought. There are several signs of hope, however. First, the correlation of intelligence, as measured by these intelligence tests, with amount of education is very high. This means that if one has more education, his intelligence tends to be higher and to stay higher longer. And the educational level of the American population has been increasing steadily over the last century.

Second, the age at which the decline in intelligence is said to begin has been rising progressively over the years of research. A generation ago, the peak of intelligence was stated as twelve, then it rose to seventeen, then to about twenty-three, then to about thirty, then fifty, and a recent report shows no significant drop before seventy.[8]

It is important to note, though, that the one function that clearly decreases throughout maturity and old age is speed, and anything involving speed—and, of course, almost everything does involve speed—will show decline early. Slowing down starts in the twenties or at least the thirties. On the other hand, capacities that involve accumulation and storage of experience, e.g., vocabulary and information, show increases throughout the life span until just before death. Thus, it now looks as if early findings about intellectual decreases (which, incidentally had been based on cross-sectional rather than the more appropriate longitudinal research) were more likely measuring secular trends in eduation of the population rather than decline in intelligence. If necessary, old people can learn new ways, particularly if given time.

It is useful to think of three kinds of aging: physical aging, social aging, and psychologic aging. They may not necessarily be in step. For example, it is possible to be physically aged in the forties, but at the same time, socially middle aged and psychologically young. A college professor who is keen of mind, at the height of social involvement, but with little physical activity would fit this description. It is equally possible to be physically middle aged in the seventies, socially young, and psychologically old. A vigorous golfer with many friends and few social responsibilities whose thinking has become rigid and slow would fit this combination. At another extreme, it is possible to be physically alive but socially and psychologically dead. This is true of old and not-so-old patients in mental hospitals, chronic hospitals, or nursing homes. It is also true of many older people living in their children's homes and having no social role or function there.

From earliest life, eating is a social activity, embedded in a complex web of interpersonal interactions and interrelationships. The baby develops love for his mother within the bounds of an eating situation and whether the enriched meaning of food comes from mother love or the enriched meaning of mother love comes from the satisfactions of eating is a moot point. All through life, enjoyment of life is wrapped up with enjoyment of food. Consider such significant food-involving situations as the family evening dinner, the birthday party, the dating dinner, the Thanksgiving get-together, the wedding breakfast, and the funeral meets. One of the consequences of losses of relatives and friends in old age is a loss of eating companions and, therefore, probably, a reduction in the enjoyment of eating.

The aged can be defined generally as anybody over the age of sixty-five, though if we wish to consider the more feeble, more disabled group, the cutting age is more appropriately seventy-five. The dividing line of sixty-five is customary because it has been set as the legal age for such signaling events as eligibility for Social Security or, in many jobs, compulsory retirement.

THE WIDOWED

While most Americans over sixty-five live in their own homes with their own husband or wife, there are many who are residentially isolated. Because, on the average, women live longer than men, there are more residentially isolated old women than old men.[1] Other factors contributing to this unequal sex distribution are the tendency for women to marry older men and the fewer chances for an old widow to find a new husband than for an old widower to find a new wife. However, in part, it is also a question to options. Old widowers remarry more than old widows because there are fewer other alternatives open to them. Old widows can take care of themselves—they are experienced housekeepers; they can move in with a relative (daughter or son, sister, or other); or they can look for a new spouse (and occasionally even find one). Old widowers usually are unprepared to take care of themselves, and most of their contacts with kin have been engineered by their wives so that they are at a loss for communication with children, siblings, and so on. The one arrangement they have been socialized for is with a wife.

Many widows live alone because they like it that way. Lopata studied[9] 301 widows, age fifty or over, in the Chicago area. Half of the sample lived alone, and the proportion increased to a peak of 61 per cent between the ages of sixty-five and sixty-nine.

There is a difference between isolation and desolation.[10] We could describe isolates as those who live alone and like it and desolates as those who live alone but don't like it. Many isolates have lived alone and been "loners" most of their lives.[11] The desolates are the ones who have loved and lost. Their spouses have died; their children live far away; and they haven't adjusted to the loneliness yet —if they ever will. They are the ones we in the helping professions must worry about.

THE DESOLATES

How many desolates are there? This cannot be ascertained directly at present. Probably the 4 per cent of those over sixty-five who are in institutions—hospitals, mental hospitals, nursing homes, retirement homes, and so forth—could be so designated.[1] But how many of the 20 per cent of those over sixty-five who live alone should be? Lowenthal compared[11] old-age admissions to the psychiatric ward of the San Francisco County General Hospital with old people living successfully in the community. She found that one of the most significant differences between the two groups was having a confidant: at least one friend who knew whether one were alive and who cared.

Residential isolation could thus be less important than communicative isolation. One could live with other people but if one had no interaction with them, if one's presence were as meaningful to them as a piece of furniture pushed into a corner, one would be more effectively isolated than if one lived alone but talked on the phone daily with a friend on the other side of town, even if one saw that friend rarely face to face.

Within the last ten or fifteen years, a number of intensive research projects on aging have been carried out. One of the earliest and most extensive was the series of Kansas City studies under the direction of the University of Chicago Committee on Human Development.[2,12,13] As the data began accumulating, they pointed to a trend of aging behavior that has been called "disengagement." This refers to a process of withdrawal from social roles and social activity by the aging person that coincides with the simultaneous rejection of the aging person by society. It is not only that society discards its "useless" aged, but that the aged no longer have much use for society.

In the original formulation of this theory, it was assumed that because disengagement was functional, both for the individual and the society, those individuals who disengaged the most would be the happiest. This has not proved to be true. It is the other way around. While there has been repeated replication of the existence of a disengagement process, it has become more and more clear that, in general, those who disengage the least—who remain the most involved in society and the most active, tend to be the most satisfied with their lives and to have the highest morale. To stay alive in the social and psychologic sense, one must act alive.[2]

This rule should not be taken too literally, however. More refined studies, both on the Kansas City data[2] and in California,[14] have shown that in the last analysis, the kind of aging pattern that is the most satisfying to a given individual is a function of his personality. Both studies show more than one type of successful aging, including those who continue to be happily engaged, those who remain engaged but "pushed themselves" because they are afraid to let go, and those who are the contented disengaged, the rocking-chair people who have been looking forward for many years to sitting back and letting others take over and who now feel they have earned their rest.

FOOD IN THE AGING PICTURE

Part of the goal of any nutrition program for older people, therefore, should be not only to keep them physically alive but also socially and psychologically alive. That means that a good nutrition program for the aged includes more than the proper balance of nourishing foods, even nourishing food adapted to the individual's past tastes and prejudices and taboos. It includes at least some opportunity for meaningful social involvement and some opportunity for individual planning and choice of both food and social involvement to suit varying personality types. Recent government-sponsored demonstration projects on the nutrition of the aged have, in fact, been paying particular attention to the multiple facets of the eating experience.[3,15]

At the beginning of this paper, some dilemmas were posed about therapeutic dietetic intervention in old age. Can we now come to any resolution? it seems that the best resolution would lie in considered judgment. Knowing that old people have survived because there was something good in the way they lived and ate, that their eating habits are tied up with what gives meaning and significance to their lives, but that they have changed physically in many cases so that old ways are now no longer so good and also that they have the capacity to change if necessary, the practitioner can balance the pros and cons and come to the wisest decision for each individual.

It could very well be that our potential life span is something we are programmed with at conception.[16,17] Furthermore, the important dietary and other environmental influences on this programming may be those that occur in the beginning of the life span.[3,18] Whether we will live out our potential life span could depend more on our mother's eating habits and her general state of health, and on her care of us in infancy than on anything we ourselves eat in middle or old age. The state of research is still primitive in this respect, but so far as can be judged now, it looks as if dietary intervention in old age is more a maintenance or holding action than a change action. Magic diets, like magic organ transplants, cannot make old men young. Reincarnation is still a religious, not a medical hypothesis.

In conclusion, let me quote from Howell and Loeb[3]: "Many doctors, nurses, social workers, and middle-aged children report that older people, especially those living alone, do not appear to eat enough or to eat a nutritionally balanced diet. However, there is little reported evidence of a high incidence of actual 'clinical' malnutrition among old adults in the United States . . . Better correlation of medical records with dietary history and subjective health reports might help to accumulate needed information on diet and the health status of the aged" (p. 63).

REFERENCES

 1. Riley, M., and Foner, A.: Aging and Society. Vol. 1. An Inventory of Research Findings, N.Y.: Russell Sage Foundation, 1968.
 2. Neugarten, B.: Middle Age and Aging: A Reader in Social Psychology. Chicago: Univ. of Chicago Press, 1968.
 3. Howell, S., and Loeb, M. B.: Nutrition and Aging. A Monograph for Practitioners. The Gerontologist **9**: No. 3, Pt. II, 1969.
 4. Birren, J. E.: The Psychology of Aging. Englewood Cliffs, N.J.: Prentice-Hall, Inc., 1964.
 5. White House Conference on Aging. Fact Sheet, Rev., June 1970.
 6. Bromley, D. B.: The Psychology of Human Aging. Baltimore: Penguin Books, 1966.
 7. Kuhlen, R.: Age and Intelligence: The Significance of Culture Change in Longitudinal vs. Cross-sectional Findings. Vita Humana **6**: No. 3, 1963.
 8. Eisdorfer, C.: Intellectual changes with advancing age: A 10-year follow-up of the Duke sample. Paper presented at a symposium on "Longitudinal Changes with Advancing Age," Amer. Psych. Assn., San Francisco, 1968.
 9. Lopata, H.: Living arrangements of American urban widows. Paper presented before Gerontological Society, Toronto, 1970.
10. Lowenthal, M., and Haven, C.: Interaction and Adaptation: Intimacy as a Critical Variable. Amer. Sociol. Rev. **33**:20, 1968.
11. Lowenthal, M.: Lives in Distress: The Paths of the Elderly to the Psychiatric Ward. N.Y.: Basic Books, 1964.
12. Cumming, E., and Henry, W.: Growing Old: The Process of Disengagement. N.Y.: Basic Books, 1961.
13. Neugarten, B., Berkowitz, H., and others: Personality in Middle and Late Life: Empirical Studies, N.Y.: Atherton Press, 1964.
14. Riechard, S., Livson, F., and Petersen, P.: Aging and Personality: A Study of Eighty-seven Older Men. N.Y.: John Wiley & Sons, 1962.
15. Pelcovits, J., and Holmes, D.: A nutrition program for Older Americans. Position paper: Nutrition for Older Americans: Demonstration Program Experience. Washington, D.C.: Admin. on Aging, n. d.
16. Comfort, A.: Theories of aging. Paper presented at 8th Intl. Cong. of Gerontology, Washington, D.C., 1969.
17. Strehler, B., ed.: The Biology of Aging. Washington, D.C.: Amer. Inst. of Biol. Sci., 1960.
18. Sherwood, S.: Gerontology and the Sociology of Food and Eating. Aging and Human Development **1**:61, 1970.

MYTHS AND REALITIES ABOUT AGED BLACKS

Jacquelyne J. Jackson, Ph.D.,* and Bertram E. Walls, M.D.**

Many self-styled advocates for aged blacks mask their vested interests in seeking racially based appropriations for federally funded programs for the aged by proclaiming that aged blacks are unique and doubly victimized by virtue of being both old and black. Economic and political struggles underlying attempts to develop a pluralistic society may well justify such polemics. Paradoxically, those very struggles also undermine the development of gerontological knowledge about blacks. Gerontological literature about blacks, still generally sparse, fragmented, and inconclusive, despite its recent proliferation, is heavily influenced by myths oozing with racial biases. Inadequate racial comparisons by some gerontologists strengthen these myths.

For example, a major issue in the literature is racial variation in the importance attached to religion by the aged. Faulty methods and racial biases generally led Stone (1959), Heyman and Jeffers (1964), Smith (1967), and Jackson and Wood (1976) to conclusions that in comparion with aged whites, religion is significantly more important to aged blacks. Jackson (1967), however, found racial similarities in comparisons of aged blacks and whites of similar socioeconomic statuses. Which view more nearly approximates reality? Such problems as inadequate sampling and statistical procedures in the studies just cited prevented any satisfactory resolution of this or related issues in the past.

*Associate Professor, Medical Sociology, Department of Psychiatry, Duke University Medical Center; Senior Fellow, Center for the Study of Aging and Human Development, Duke University, Durham, North Carolina.
**Resident, Department of Obstetrics-Gynecology, Duke University Medical Center; formerly Postdoctoral Fellow, Center for the Study of Aging and Human Development, Duke University, Durham, North Carolina.

PURPOSE AND METHODS

Fortunately, the recent availability of data tapes from the Harris and associates' (1975) survey of aging attitudes and behaviors among the 1974 adult population of the United States now permits their examination, a task already undertaken inadequately and too hastily by Jackson and Wood (1976). They imputed significant differences by race merely on the basis of differentials of 10 percentage points, a highly inappropriate procedure.

For example, Jackson and Wood (1976) found that 84% of the black but only 70% of the white aged regarded religion as being "very important." Believing in the centrality of religion in black communities, they then concluded that religion was significantly more important for black than white aged.

Other conclusions they reached are circumspect in some instances because of inadequate knowledge about aged blacks and whites. For example, they erroneously attributed greater widowhood among black than white aged to higher sex ratios among aged whites than aged blacks. Yet, as in the past, although the gaps continue to narrow, the proportion of men in the aged black population remains greater than that within the aged white population.

Hence, although Jackson and Wood (1976) reported many similarities between aged blacks and whites in the Harris sample, concern should focus heavily on the racial differences to which they imputed significance, such as those related to the importance that the aged attached to religion.

The major purpose of this chapter, then, is to shed some further light on racial myths about aged blacks and whites and to set forth certain implications of that light for aging programs involving blacks. Contrasts between aged (65 or more years of age) blacks and whites as well as between young (18 to 64 years of age) blacks and whites are provided in the major areas of (1) sociodemographic characteristics, (2) aging images and attitudes, (3) aging activities, (4) aging problems, and (5) patterns of familial assistance.

Our analyses (largely using chi-square and t) were based on the weighted Harris sample of 3997 blacks and whites (see Harris and associates, 1975, for methodological details of the survey). We subdivided the sample initially by four race-age groups: (1) aged blacks (N = 51); (2) aged whites (N = 561); (3) young blacks (N = 374); (4) young whites (N = 3011). Aged blacks and whites were compared, and, in separate analyses, young blacks and whites were compared.

When significance (at least at the .05 level of confidence) emerged on given variables in comparisons of aged blacks and whites, comparable race-age-income groups were analyzed. Using the 1973 household income, low income and high income were dichotomized as under $4000 and $4000+ for the aged and under $7000 and $7000+ for the young. Insufficient occupational data, incidentally, led to the use of income as a socioeconomic proxy. The eight race-age-income groups were (1) low-income (N = 33) and (2) high income (N = 15) aged blacks, (3) low-income (N = 190) and (4) high-income (N = 340) aged whites, (5) low-income (N = 108) and (6) high-income (N =251) young blacks, and (7) low-income (N = 151) and (8) high-income (N = 2776) young whites.

We regard the differences that remained significant when the race-age-income groups were compared in pairs (for example, low-income aged blacks and whites) as significant only temporarily. The small size of the weighted sample of aged blacks prevented any large-scale multivariate analyses. For example, it was not possible to compare high-income aged black and white women who were college-educated and whose major lifetime occupations (or those of their spouses) were professional or managerial. In other words, we believe that most, if not all, of the significant racial differences we have reported will wash out in future research controlled for period effects. To digress briefly, we suspect that most gerontologists emphasizing racial differences in aging (for example, Bengtson and associates, 1977) need to apply more stringent socioeconomic and period controls. In any case, we are also cognizant of the fact that the small size of the aged black sample in the Harris survey prevents the detection of significant differences at a high level of probability. Therefore some differences that appeared to be insignificant in our analyses may, in fact, be significant. We cannot tell.

The representativeness of the Harris black samples may also be questioned, an issue we deal with only in illustrative form. We treated the Harris data as if they were representative, since such a pursuit helps to identify needed explanatory studies for enhancing our knowledge and understanding of aging factors among blacks, as well as racial similarities and dissimilarities between aging individuals and populations.

Specific data were generally available for each subject for all the variables in the following discussions.

SOCIODEMOGRAPHIC CHARACTERISTICS

Table 1 contains data about age, geographical location, education, occupation, employment, and income of the race-age groups and, on occasion, the race-age-income groups. The mean ages of the low-income black and white aged, as well as the high-income black and white aged and the high-income young blacks and whites, were similar. Low-income young blacks were significantly younger than the low-income young whites.

The two measures of geographical location available for this sample were region (South, East, Midwest, and West) and size (central city, town, suburban, and rural). As is also evident in Table 1, a bare majority of aged blacks in the Harris sample were in the South. According to the 1970 census, about 65% of all aged blacks lived in the South, suggesting either sampling inadequacies or significant regional shifts over time.

Significant geographical variations by region and size separated both the aged blacks and whites and the young blacks and whites. Comparisons of race-age-income groups, however, removed any significant regional differences between

Table 1. Selected sociodemographic characteristics of aged and young blacks and whites

Characteristics	Aged		Young	
	Black	White	Black	White
Age (in years)				
Low income: Mean	72.9	74.3	34.7*	41.3*
Standard deviation	6.5	6.5	14.8	17.4
High income: Mean	71.1	72.4	38.0	38.7
Standard deviation	5.6	6.1	12.1	13.5
Geographical location (%)				
Region				
South	50.5†	27.0†	33.7*	26.1*
East	31.1	31.4	26.0	29.7
Midwest	14.4	27.8	28.2	28.8
West	4.0	13.8	12.1	15.4
Size				
Central city	49.5†	28.6†	80.8*	22.5*
Town	11.8	22.1	8.0	31.0
Suburban	6.6	18.3	0.8	17.2
Rural	32.1	31.0	10.4	29.2
Female (%)	57.7	59.3	55.1	52.5
Educational level (%)				
Low income				
Less than high school	89.8†	57.9†	23.1*	24.5
Completed high school only	8.1	32.9	73.2	35.1
Post–high school	2.1	9.2	3.6	40.5
High income				
Less than high school	54.7	35.2	21.1*	7.9
Completed high school only	25.9	36.9	52.5	47.2
Post–high school	19.3	27.9	26.3	44.8
Occupation (labor force or retired) (%)				
Professional, managerial	7.1†	24.6	13.0*	29.3
Clerical, sales	2.3	17.7	14.3	19.8
Skilled	8.9	19.3	19.4	23.0
All other	81.7	38.3	53.2	27.9
Employment (%)				
Employed full or part-time	11.0	12.3	63.5*	57.6*
Unemployed	7.3	5.0	16.2	9.4
Retired	69.9	62.5	4.6	4.8
Student, housewife	9.5	18.2	14.5	26.6
1973 household income (%)				
Under $4000	68.6†	35.8†	30.0*	5.2*
$4000 to 6999	20.5	29.4	15.6	10.0
$7000 to $9999	6.3	16.3	17.0	15.4
$10,000+	4.6	18.4	37.3	69.4

*Young blacks and whites differed significantly on this variable.
†Aged blacks and whites differed significantly on this variable.

the high-income black and white aged and between the high-income young blacks and whites. Also removed were any significant differences by size between low-income aged blacks and whites.

The majority of the respondents within each race-age group were, as expected, female, with the female proportion being somewhat higher among the aged than the young.

When paired race-age-income groups were compared, the high-income aged blacks and whites were indistinguishable by educational level. Comparisons between the remaining paired groups, however, produced the usual findings favoring whites, due partially to our gross educational categories.

The occupational distributions for those still within or retired from the labor force by race and age were also not unexpected. Blacks were typically overrepresented within the lower and whites within the upper occupational levels. Within this sample, both employment and unemployment were significantly higher among the young blacks than the young whites, which may reflect the historical tendency of somewhat greater female participation in the labor force among blacks than whites. The aged were racially indistinguishable by employment patterns, including, incidentally, being forced to or choosing to retire.

Table I, shows that about 69% of the aged blacks but only 39% of the aged whites were in households where the 1973 household income was under $4000, with similar data being about 30% for young blacks and 5% for young whites. However, although poverty was dominant among aged blacks, *not all aged blacks were poor, just as not all young whites were wealthy. Race and age alone do not determine poverty.*

The largest single source of income for both the black (87%) and white (61%) aged was Social Security. Black dependence on Social Security was not significantly greater than white dependence. That is, the high-income black and white aged were statistically indistinguishable on this variable. Among the low-income aged, however, blacks were significantly more likely than whites to indicate that Social Security was their largest single source of income. Yet a majority of both low-income black and white aged depended heavily on Social Security.

Such data about Social Security, coupled with significant changes in the composition of the aging black population and social factors affecting that population, led Jackson (1968, 1971) to withdraw recently her "Social Security proposal" about differential minimum-age eligibility requirements for black and white men as primary beneficiaries of OASDHI.*

Table 2 contains data about various marital, familial, and friendship patterns of the groups. As expected (see, for example, Jackson, 1970), insignificant differences characterized the marital statuses of both the low-income and the high-income aged blacks and whites. A minority of the low-income groups were mar-

---

*Old Age Survivors Disability and Health Insurance, now known as SSI (Supplemental Social Income).

Table 2. Selected marital, familial, and friendship patterns of the aged and young blacks and whites (in percent)

Characteristics	Aged		Young	
	Black	White	Black	White
Marital status				
Low-income				
Single	3.3	4.5	44.1*	31.7*
Married, with spouse	37.6	38.8	32.1	35.4
Separated, divorced	4.9	3.5	16.6	13.3
Widowed	54.2	53.1	7.2	19.6
High-income				
Single	2.2	4.6	15.6*	19.7*
Married, with spouse	58.4	66.1	62.5	78.4
Separated, divorced	9.1	1.6	14.5	4.1
Widowed	30.3	27.7	3.3	1.9
No children under 12 years of age in household	90.8†	97.4†	50.6*	59.7*
No children 12 to 17 years old in household	91.6	97.4	55.1*	72.0*
Number of living children				
None	28.5	18.9	30.2	25.6
One or two	34.7	46.4	35.3	39.5
Three or more	36.8	34.8	34.5	34.9
Number of living siblings				
None	25.7	20.2	9.5	9.0
One or two	38.4	44.5	40.0	45.7
Three or more	36.0	35.3	50.5	45.3
Number of living parents				
None	97.6	95.8	41.0*	29.8
One	2.3	4.2	32.4	28.7
Two	0.1	0.1	26.7	41.4
Number of living grandchildren (aged) or living grandparents (young)				
None	33.2	24.4	73.9†	70.8
Number of close friends				
None	9.3	5.2	7.2†	2.5
One or two	15.4	7.4	19.3	7.3
Three or four	11.3	9.7	23.2	13.8
Five or more	64.0	77.6	50.3	76.4

*Young blacks and whites differed significantly on this variable.
†Aged blacks and whites differed significantly on this variable.

ried and living with their spouses, with the reverse being true of the high-income groups. In general, the higher their socioeconomic status, the greater the likelihood of having a spouse present.

Divergent patterns in marital statuses by race represent a recent phenomenon (Jackson, 1973). The pattern was not borrowed from slavery. Among younger blacks in particular, it is a partial function of the diminishing sex ratio as well as sex differences in geographical location of employment attractions. Incidentally, we did not age-adjust the marital data for racial comparisons.

It may appear that aged blacks and whites and young blacks and whites differed significantly by the presence of children under 12 years of age within their households. However, a comparison of the race-age-income groups among the aged removed any significant differences. For example, low-income aged blacks were no more likely and no less likely than low-income aged whites to have such children within their households. Income controls did not, however, erase the significant differences by race among the young due, no doubt, to age and income differences within the subsample.

Aged blacks and whites and young blacks and whites also were similar by the number of living children and siblings. A majority in each group had at least one living child and/or sibling. Few of the aged blacks and whites had any living parents; young whites were generally more likely than young blacks to report living parents. A majority of the aged—somewhat higher among whites—had at least one living grandchild. More than two thirds of the young groups—significantly higher among blacks—did not have at least one living grandparent.

Most in all of the race-age groups reported five or more close friends. Insignificant differences characterized the aged blacks and whites. Among the young, whites were significantly more likely to report the presence of more numerous close friends.

AGING IMAGES AND ATTITUDES

Most aged blacks and whites had good self-images. They considered themselves friendly and warm, wise from experience, bright and alert, and open minded and adaptable. Almost half said they were good at getting things done. About a third believed they were physically active. About 12% said they were also active sexually. In contrast, their images of most aged persons were more negative, a not uncommon psychological phenomenon.

A similar pattern generally prevailed among the young. They also tended to characterize themselves more favorably than they did most aged persons. However, they tended to consider aged persons as friendlier, warmer, and wiser than themselves. The images of aged persons by the aged (exclusive of themselves) and the young were similar and typically negative. Aside from young blacks being decidedly less likely than young whites to depict aged persons as bright and alert (although a majority did), no significant racial differences emerged here.

The use of nonchronological referents in determining when women and men are old was typical across the race-age groups. Also similar, regardless of race and age, was the tendency to depict the best years of one's life as occurring in the middle or earlier years, with the worst years coinciding more closely with the later years.

Most respondents knew about recent age shifts within the American population. Most thought that the socioeconomic and health statuses of the aged had improved over time. Most also knew that the proportion of aged persons living alone was increasing. The few differences that seemed to have been racial were actually functions of socioeconomic variables.

Little agreement about an identifying term for the group of aged persons existed. The modal term *senior citizen* was endorsed only by a minority within each race-age group. This lack of consensus suggests that the aged do *not* consider themselves as a minority group, despite current efforts to make them such.

Most black and white aged persons believed that aged persons received insufficient respect from the young, and the young generally agreed. Racial differences across income groups were similar, suggesting especially that low-income aged parents are more concerned about respect from their family and friends, whereas high-income aged parents are more concerned about love (see, for example, Jackson, 1971). A minority of the groups thought that young persons received sufficient respect from the aged, with which the aged also tended to agree.

Age preferences for human associations and age-integrated housing patterns revealed some racial and socioeconomic differences. Specifically, the low-income young blacks and whites were distinguishable in that most of the blacks preferred associations with persons similar in age. Among the high-income young, most, regardless of race, preferred associations with persons of different ages, a pattern somewhat more pronounced among the whites. The low-income and high-income black and white aged groups were similar in desiring associations with persons of varied ages. Aged blacks and whites were also similar in preferring age-integrated and age-segregated housing. Neither pattern was clearly favored by any aged group.

Most of the Harris respondents were Protestants. When dichotomized by Protestant and non-Protestant, only the low-income aged blacks and whites and the low-income young blacks and whites differed significantly by religious affiliation. Almost all the blacks were Protestants.

Even without income controls, the aged blacks and whites in this sample did *not* differ significantly by their assessment of the importance of religion. Young blacks, however, tended to attach greater importance to religion than did young whites, even when the income controls employed in this study were used to analyze the relevant data. The associations between socioeconomic status and importance attached to religion clearly deserve more study. Within this sample, low-income young blacks and whites were somewhat less likely than their respective high-income counterparts to consider religion as important.

Contrary to popular belief, most aged persons, black or white, do not wish to work. Many who indicated an interest in work doubted seriously whether they would accept available and adequate employment. Some aged who indicated a preference for working really seek income supplementation. Others may feel

Table 3. Actual preparation and importance of preparation for later life by aged and young blacks and whites (in percent)

| | Have done | | | | Important to do | | | |
| | Aged | | Young | | Aged | | Young | |
Preparation tasks	Blacks	Whites	Blacks	Whites	Blacks	Whites	Blacks	Whites
Certain of available medical care	77.3	90.4	36.4	58.4*	89.9	86.3	70.1	90.7
Learned about pensions or Social Security benefits	72.8	89.6	39.2	47.1*	82.4	86.9	63.6	82.1
Decided about residential site in old age	63.6	75.9	42.0	48.1	50.6	58.2	47.4	52.3
Bought own home	50.3	76.7	39.2	63.7*†	72.4	77.6	57.3	71.9
Talked to older people about what it is like to grow old	46.9	34.8	34.0	27.2†	41.9	28.1	33.9	24.2
Developed hobbies or leisure-time activities	42.6	66.1	31.8	59.4	46.9	63.7	46.8	68.2*†
Built up own savings	36.3	78.4†	33.2	44.9*	83.8	86.5	67.4	81.4
Prepared will	30.5	68.1†	19.2	34.5*	56.9	83.3†	56.7	86.6*
Moved in with children or other relatives	12.4	9.1	9.2	3.5	14.3	6.4†	14.5	4.4*†
Planned new part-time or full-time job	11.1	16.2	12.2	15.1	31.8	28.1	35.8	31.9
Enrolled in retirement counseling or preparatory program	8.0	8.2	12.1	6.5	32.4	20.2	32.6	22.1

*Chi-square results based on 2df or 3df showed significant differences at least at .05 between high-income aged blacks and whites or high-income young blacks and whites. Percentages shown in each case were those prior to income controls. That is, they are for race-age groups.

†Chi-square results based on 2df or 3df showed significant differences at least at .05 between low-income aged blacks and whites or low-income young blacks and whites. Percentages shown in each case were those prior to income controls. That is, they are for race-age groups.

compelled to support the Protestant Ethic. In any case, aged blacks and whites do not vary significantly in their desire to work.

Table 3 shows that differences between aged blacks and whites by retirement preparation or the importance of that preparation were functions largely of socio-economic status. Low-income aged blacks and whites differed significantly in that fewer of the former had drawn up wills, and more had moved in with children or other relatives. Furthermore, a significantly larger proportion of the low-income aged whites than the low-income aged blacks thought it was important to draw up a will.

Jackson and Wood (1976) contended that significant racial differences among the aged existed with respect to the acquisition of medical care, knowledge about pensions and Social Security benefits, home ownership, the development of leisure-time activities, building up savings, and preparation of a will, but, in general, our analyses do not support their contentions, as already suggested. The major differences in preparing for retirement by these tasks are *not* racial. They are, instead, socioeconomic.

It is worth noting, however, that a majority of aged blacks did place great value on building up their savings and preparing a will, but only a minority were able to follow through. These discrepancies were far less common among the white aged.

Racial differences in preparation for retirement and in values about the importance of such preparation were more pronounced among the young blacks and whites, as may also be seen in Table 3. Since these differences tended to be more characteristic of the high-income groups, it is reasonable to assume that most of them are functions of socioeconomic status. For example, during the past several decades, racial differences in the ability to purchase housing have decreased considerably. The extant racial differences now more nearly relate to the quality and location of homes that can be purchased.

Most of the respondents, regardless of race, age, and income, believed that volunteer organizations should work toward improving the statuses of aged persons in the United States. However, only a minority thought that they, themselves, would become a part of such a citizens' group. When controlled for income, blacks were no more certain that they would join such an organization than were whites.

AGING ACTIVITIES

Table 4 shows the percentage of persons in each race-age group who rarely, if ever, participated in the listed activities, as well as their perceptions of the frequency of participation in such activities by most aged persons. It also shows the judgments about locational convenience of various places to the subjects and whether they had visited such places within the year preceding the interview.

When controlled for income, no significant differences separated aged blacks and whites by participation in the listed activities. A Spearman rho correlation

Table 4. Participation in activities, perceptions of participation by aged persons, and convenience of location of facilities for aged and young blacks and whites (in percent)

Characteristics	Personally				Perceptions of aged			
	Aged		Young		Aged		Young	
	Blacks	Whites	Blacks	Whites	Blacks	Whites	Blacks	Whites
Activities: spending hardly any time at all								
Participating in sports	95.0	88.8	52.2	48.6	62.6	54.8	48.6	59.3
Doing volunteer work	81.8	76.3	56.4	67.0	35.3	31.6	36.8	28.6*†
Working full or part-time	77.4	76.8	29.0	33.5	42.5	45.0	39.5	52.3
Participating in political activities	76.7	75.0	59.4	73.4	39.9	37.3	40.4	46.1
Participating in fraternities, community organizations, clubs	67.0	60.7	47.4	58.3	31.8	20.7	35.7	18.6
Participating in recreational activities and hobbies	63.1	45.3	32.5	23.9*†	34.4	18.7*	32.8	19.2*†
Caring for family members	49.3	50.6	20.2	22.6	18.3	24.7	18.5	27.0
Gardening, raising plants	44.6	34.8	47.8	32.1	16.7	12.7	17.8	6.5
Reading	43.9	24.2	24.7	17.3*†	19.1	9.3	16.8	4.8*†
Just sitting and thinking	38.1	60.1	17.6	24.2*	3.3	10.7	8.4	4.6
Just doing nothing	38.1	60.1	42.7	67.7*†	10.7	24.5	15.2	18.4
Going for walks	34.5	41.3	39.5	39.5	15.5	18.3	16.0	10.7
Sleeping	24.0	33.5	12.1	23.7	6.7	12.5	8.5	9.7
Watching television	16.4	18.0	7.2	28.5	3.2	2.7	5.0	3.4
Socializing with friends	13.7	13.5	4.5	6.1	9.9	6.3	7.6	4.1

*Chi-square results based on 2df or 3df showed significant differences at least at .05 between low-income aged blacks and whites or low-income young blacks and whites. Percentages shown in each case were those prior to income controls. This is, they are for race-age groups.

†Chi-square results based on 2df or 3df showed significant differences at least at .05 between high-income aged blacks and whites or high-income young blacks and whites. Percentages shown in each case were those prior to income controls. That is, they are for race-age groups.

Continued.

Table 4. Participation in activities, perceptions of participation by aged persons, and convenience of location of facilities for aged and young blacks and whites (in percent)—cont'd

Characteristics	Convenience				Visited within past year			
	Aged		Young		Aged		Young	
	Blacks	Whites	Blacks	Whites	Blacks	Whites	Blacks	Whites
Convenience and visitation								
Home of neighbor	92.8	94.7	97.6	98.4	87.9	85.1	93.3	92.4
Church	91.4	90.9	93.5	98.0	87.1	76.1	77.2	74.4
Places to shop	79.0	86.8	84.9	96.5	84.8	90.3	91.7	97.9
Doctor or clinic	75.4	84.2	86.9	96.1	82.3	82.1	81.3	85.7
Home of relative	71.2	78.8	81.8	83.9	79.5	85.6	90.7	92.6
Restaurant	62.8	81.6	77.8	96.8	41.3	71.5*	78.2	93.2
Public park	46.5	63.4	79.6	87.2	27.3	31.2	67.1	67.7
Community, neighborhood, or recreation center	42.4	45.6	68.9	62.8	21.9	17.1	50.1	33.9
Sports event	25.9	46.7	63.4	82.2	16.2	19.6	58.4	59.7
Museum	20.1	36.1	54.2	60.2	10.5	19.2	31.7	42.7
Live theater, dance, musical concert	17.8	34.8	54.3	62.4	10.6	18.1	46.0	46.6

of .867 (significant beyond the .01 level) was strongest between the aged black and white pairs, although the associations were also significant between the pairs of aged and young blacks, aged and young whites, and young blacks and whites.

The use of income controls also contradicted Jackson and Wood's (1976) contentions that aged blacks were significantly less likely than aged whites to participate in reading, recreational activities and hobbies, fraternities, community organizations, and clubs. Contrary to their view as well, income controls erased the racial differences in locational convenience of restaurants, although, among low-income aged, the whites were still significantly more likely to have visited a restaurant within the past year. Even without income controls, aged blacks and whites were not significantly different by visits to homes of neighbors and frequency of church attendance. In the latter instance, racial differences were not even apparent when the data were analyzed by frequency of church attendance within the week preceding the interview.

Among the young, both the low-income and high-income blacks were significantly less likely than their white counterparts to participate in recreational activities and hobbies and to read, and they were significantly more likely to just do nothing. The low-income blacks were also significantly more likely than the low-income whites among the young to just sit and think.

The aged blacks and whites varied significantly only by their perceptions of the participation of other aged persons in recreational activities and hobbies. Racial variations in perceptions of the aged by the young existed within both income groups by volunteer work, participation in recreational activities and hobbies, and reading.

As in the earlier comparison of self-ratings and ratings of aged persons by these Harris subjects, both the aged and the young, regardless of race, generally perceived themselves more favorably than they did others. In this instance, they typically thought they were more active than most aged persons.

The data about attending church, visiting neighbors and relatives, and shopping during the week preceding the interview help provide fuel against the stereotype of isolation of the aged. Except for aged blacks, a majority of all of the subjects reported being in a restuarant within the past week as well, thus indicating drastic changes in American life-style over the century.

About a third of each group reported visiting a doctor or clinic during the past week. The greater percentage of black visitation here, however, should not necessarily be interpreted as blacks being in poorer health than whites. When controlled for income, no significant racial differences emerged.

AGING PROBLEMS

The subjects were asked to consider the seriousness of various problems for them and for most aged persons. As shown in Table 5, the personal halo effect also operated here. Problems were perceived to be less serious for the subjects,

Table 5. Perceptions of problems for self and for most people 65 or more years of age by aged and young blacks and whites (in percent)

Hardly a problem	For self				For most aged			
	Aged		Young		Aged		Young	
	Blacks	Whites	Blacks	Whites	Blacks	Whites	Blacks	Whites
Not enough friends	78.5	85.8	69.6	91.7	25.5	22.4	20.3	25.1
Not enough clothing	73.6	95.0*	67.0	92.4*†	42.6	25.6	29.3	45.2*†
Not feeling needed	72.0	81.7	72.3	89.9	14.6	12.0	12.6	8.6
Not enough job opportunities	70.3	89.3*	53.0	75.5*†	17.3	29.4	23.6	23.2
Not enough to do to keep busy	66.6	85.1	72.8	90.5*†	16.8	20.6	18.2	15.9
Poor housing	62.9	92.4*	55.4	91.5*†	11.8	19.4	12.8	21.1
Loneliness	55.4	72.3	68.0	83.0†	7.0	6.2	8.9	5.0
Not enough medical care	52.5	79.3*	65.5	84.1†	16.7	24.0	19.0	19.4
Not enough education	42.2	78.2*	43.5	75.9*†	10.2	28.1*	20.6	39.9*†
Fear of crime	34.5	54.0	42.5	65.8*†	10.5	14.9	6.6	12.4
Poor health	30.4	52.0	56.9	80.1†	11.8	19.4	6.6	4.5
Not enough money to live on	24.7	64.1*	34.0	54.4†	4.6	9.0	5.5	4.8
Cost of buses or subways	27.6	24.3	16.4	21.5	69.5	81.3	58.3	89.2
Not having a car or being able to drive	24.8	15.8	16.6	11.0	70.0	76.7	58.5	90.7
No buses or subways for preferred destination	19.2	23.4	20.5	16.3	65.6	75.8	62.0	82.8
Danger of being robbed or attacked on street	11.2	14.0	6.4	14.0	35.0	57.9†	40.9	73.6*†
Difficulty in walking and climbing stairs	8.5	9.2	7.1	5.6	34.2	55.8	63.0	90.0*†
General health	7.7	8.4	6.6	5.9	37.5	53.7	61.3	85.6†

*Chi-square results based on 2df or 3df showed significant differences at least at .05 between the low-income aged blacks and whites or low-income young blacks and whites. Percentages shown in each case were those prior to income controls. That is, they are for the race-age groups.
†Chi-square results based on 2df or 3df showed significant differences at least at .05 between the high-income aged blacks and whites or high-income young blacks and whites. Percentages shown in each case were those prior to income controls. That is, they are for the race-age groups.

aged or young, than for most aged persons. The high-income aged blacks and whites had similar perceptions about the seriousness of problems of insufficient friends, clothing, usefulness, job opportunities, activities to keep busy, housing, loneliness, medical care, education, fear of crime, health, finances, and transportation. In comparison to low-income aged whites, low-income aged blacks were significantly more likely to state that they had serious problems with clothing, job opportunities, housing, medical care, education, and money. However, only a minority of the low-income aged blacks considered clothing, job opportunities, housing, and medical care as serious problems.

Significant racial differences remaining among the young when our income controls were applied were generally similar to those between the low-income aged blacks and whites. Both the low-income and high-income young blacks were far more likely than their white counterparts to have had serious problems with clothing, job opportunities, keeping busy, housing, education, and crime protection. Among the high-income young, blacks were significantly more likely to view loneliness, health, medical care, and finances as serious problems.

We emphasize again the likelihood that the types of racial differences suggested above are spurious. However, we are particularly intrigued by the data about loneliness. Our pilot study of menopausal behaviors and attitudes among black women (Walls and Jackson, 1977) showed loneliness as the most important predictor of seeking medical aid by menopausal black women.

What deserves most emphasis in this chapter, perhaps, is the keen need of low-income young and aged blacks for better education, housing, clothing, and medical care, and for more money. In general, however, they share such problems with low-income young and aged whites. That is, the similarity between low-income aged blacks and whites and low-income young blacks and whites is far greater than that, say, between low-income and high-income aged blacks.

FAMILY PATTERNS OF ASSISTANCE

Table 6 shows various patterns of mutual family assistance. The help from family flows from parents or grandparents to their children or grandchildren, or the reverse thereof.

With respect to help from family, almost no racial differences existed. Specifically, among the high-income groups, only advice about childrearing is more common among the blacks. Advice in varying categories was the distinguishing factor between the low-income age groups by race.

Appropriate income controls showed that aged blacks and whites were indistinguishable by help given to family with one exception. High-income aged blacks were significantly more likely than their white counterparts to give money to their families. No significant differences emerged between the low-income aged blacks and whites. High-income young blacks and whites were significantly different in that the former were far more likely to help their families with money and advice about home management. Low-income young whites were signifi-

Table 6. Help received from family and help given to family by aged and young blacks and whites (in percent)

Helping patterns	Help from family* Aged		Young		Help to family* Aged		Young	
	Blacks	Whites	Blacks	Whites	Blacks	Whites	Blacks	Whites
Giving you (them) gifts	77.1	92.4	81.9	81.7	88.3	96.7	88.0	94.9†
Helping when someone is ill	73.7	68.9	76.9	49.7	79.3	74.6	68.5	74.1
Giving (receiving) general advice on dealing with some of life's problems	65.4	37.5†	62.6	54.5‡	34.3	23.0	31.9	30.7
Giving advice on rearing children	57.2	21.7†‡	61.6‡	35.4	—	—	—	—
Taking care of small children	53.6	58.6	56.1	37.5	—	—	—	—
Giving advice on running your (their) home	42.4	19.3†	39.0	39.2	27.8	12.3	25.2	10.3‡
Helping out with money	41.7	46.0	54.0	27.7	49.7	19.9	55.8	23.3
Giving advice on job or business matters	34.0	17.9	47.8	21.1	18.7	13.0	38.9	11.8
Shop or run errands for you (them)	31.6	34.0	52.5	22.6	72.7	69.6	76.4	70.3
Help fix things around house or keep house for you (them)	31.3	25.8	28.3	18.1	58.3	55.8	58.9	60.5
Take grandchildren, nieces and nephews into home to live	28.5	16.5	43.5	16.8	—	—	—	—
Take them places, such as shopping, doctor, church	—	—	—	—	61.9	58.2	77.7	60.0
Giving advice on money matters	—	—	—	—	40.7	23.4‡	43.1	17.7‡

*Weighted Ns for items about familial assistance dropped considerably here, due largely to inapplicability of the variables for many subjects. In general, weighted Ns for *Help from family* were 32 (aged blacks), 412 (aged whites), 88 (young blacks), and 928 (young whites). For *Help to family*, the weighted Ns were 32 (aged blacks), 412 (aged whites), 42 (young blacks), and 797 (young whites).

†Chi-square results based on 2df or 3df showed significant differences at least at .05 between low-income aged blacks and whites or low-income young blacks and whites. Percentages shown in each case were those prior to income controls. That is, they are for race-age groups.

‡Chi-square results based on 2df or 3df showed significant differences at least at .05 between high-income aged blacks and whites or high-income young blacks and whites.

cantly more likely to give gifts to their families than were low-income young blacks.

More than 90% of each race-age group reported having visited their friends within the past week or two. Most saw their friends more frequently than they did their relatives, including their children, grandchildren, and siblings. The absence of racial differences in this respect is striking but not surprising to those with adequate knowledge about black and white subcultures in the United States.

Summary scores about social involvement, psychological well-being, and life satisfaction of the subjects in the various race-age-income groups were

Table 7. T values for social involvement, psychological well-being, and life satisfaction scores for paired race-age-income groups

Measures and paired groups	N	Mean	S.D.	t	df
Social involvement scores					
Low-income aged blacks	32	10.9	5.1	1.76	215
Low-income aged whites	184	12.6	4.8		
High-income aged blacks	15	11.6	4.6	0.65	349
High-income aged whites	336	12.4	4.8		
Low-income young blacks	103	10.0	4.4	3.02*	249
Low-income young whites	147	11.8	4.4		
High-income young blacks	240	11.6	4.7	4.95*	2952
High-income young whites	2713	13.2	4.6		
Psychological well-being scores					
Low-income aged blacks	33	12.2	4.3	1.13	221
Low-income aged whites	190	13.0	4.2		
High-income aged blacks	15	13.6	3.8	0.80	354
High-income aged whites	340	14.4	3.8		
Low-income young blacks	108	11.0	4.0	3.49*	257
Low-income young whites	151	12.6	3.7		
High-income young blacks	251	13.9	3.6	1.90	3026
High-income young whites	2776	14.4	3.4		
Life satisfaction scores					
Low-income aged blacks	33	22.4	9.0	1.05	221
Low-income aged whites	190	20.8	8.0		
High-income aged blacks	15	23.0	7.9	1.70	354
High-income aged whites	340	26.2	7.0		
Low-income young blacks	105	20.2	7.2	3.38*	255
Low-income young whites	151	23.4	7.4		
High-income young blacks	251	24.7	7.1	5.73*	3026
High-income young whites	2776	27.3	6.8		

*Chi-square results based on 1df or 2df showed significant differences at least at .05 between low-income aged blacks and whites or low-income young blacks and whites.

analyzed. Table 7 contains t-test values for the paired race-age-income groups under investigation. The low-income aged blacks and whites were indistinguishable by these measures, as were the high-income aged blacks and whites. The low-income young blacks and whites differed significantly by all three measures, with social involvement, psychological well-being, and life satisfaction all higher among the whites. The high-income young blacks and whites had only insignificant differences in psychological well-being but differed significantly in social involvement and life satisfaction. As is apparent, whites were also significantly higher on those two measures. We plan additional analyses of these data in the future.

CONCLUSION

The development of gerontological knowledge about blacks has been hampered severely by racial biases and vested interests. The significant differences between aged blacks and whites typically stressed by advocates for aged blacks are largely myths. Gerontologists have generally abetted the perpetuation of these myths through ineffectual controls of the variable of race in their contrasts of aged blacks and whites.

This study, which was primarily concerned with the resolution of prevalent myths about aged blacks and whites, was based on an analysis of the 1974 Harris data about aging attitudes and behaviors in the United States. The finding of a general absence of any significant racial differences between paired groups of low- and high-income aged and young blacks and whites in the Harris survey suggested strongly the vast similarity of aging processes and patterns among American blacks and whites.

An examination of variables related to sociodemographic characteristics, aging images and attitudes, aging activities, aging problems, and patterns of familial assistance showed striking similarities between low-income, as well as high-income, aged blacks and whites. For example, comparisons of appropriately controlled groups of aged blacks and whites by income levels indicated insignificant differences by such variables as activities, instrumental assistance from and to families, religion, and health. The few significant differences reported herein would undoubtedly wash out with more stringent controls for socioeconomic status. In other words, current myths about significant differences between aged blacks and whites have little, if any, validity.

The resolution of these kinds of unwarranted myths about aged blacks and whites should help pave the way for more appropriate gerontological studies of aging blacks. As an instance, the types of studies undertaken by Nowlin (1977) and Jericho (1977) are steps in the right direction. In his longitudinal comparisons of the health statuses of aged blacks and whites, Nowlin (1977) found no significant racial differences. In her longitudinal examination of changes in religious attitudes and activities among aged blacks, Jericho (1977) isolated factors distinguishing aged blacks with stable and unstable religious patterns.

We would be perplexed by the action of the National Council on Aging in publishing prematurely the Jackson and Wood (1976) study if we did not have some understanding of the intrusion of politics on the world of knowledge. Still, we deplore that action, largely because it is likely to have adverse impacts in the long run on aged blacks.

Thus the most important implication of our study for aging programs involving blacks is the need to structure such programs on adequate knowledge about the conditions under which race is and is not a factor. Furthermore, advocates for racially separated programs should avoid hiding behind aged blacks when they are clearly more concerned about building black power bases for themselves. Finally, aging training programs should place greater emphasis on training individuals of various races to provide services to individuals of various races. They should also aid their students in distinguishing clearly between significant differences between populations, such as aged blacks and whites, and significant differences between individuals who happen to be aged blacks or whites.

REFERENCES

Bengtson, V. L., Kasschau, P. L., and Ragan, P. K. The impact of social structure on aging individuals. In Birren, J. E., and Schaie (Eds.). In *Handbook of the psychology of aging*. New York: Van Nostrand Reinhold Co., 1977, pp. 327-354.

Harris, Louis, and associates. *The myth and reality of aging in America*. Washington, D.C.: National Council on the Aging, 1975.

Heyman, D., and Jeffers, F. Study of the relative influence of race and socioeconomic status upon the activities and attitudes of a southern aged population. *Journal of Gerontology*, 1964, **19**, 225-229.

Jackson, J. Social gerontology and the Negro: a review. *The Gerontologist*, 1967, **7**, 168-178.

Jackson, J. Aged Negroes: their cultural departures from stereotypes and rural-urban differences. Paper presented at the 1968 annual meeting of the Gerontological Society, Denver, Colorado.

Jackson, J. Aged Negroes: their cultural departures from statistical stereotypes and selected rural-urban differences. *The Gerontologist*, 1970, **10**, 140-145.

Jackson, J. Aged blacks; a potpourri in the direction of the reduction of inequities. *Phylon*, 1971, **32**, 269-280.

Jackson, J. Black women in a racist society. In Willie, C. V., Kramer, B., and Brown, B. (Eds.). *Racism and mental health*. Pittsburgh: University of Pittsburgh Press, 1973.

Jackson, M., and Wood, J. L. *Aging in America: implications for the black aged*. Washington, D.C.: National Council on the Aging, 1976.

Jericho, B. Longitudinal changes in religious activity subscores of aged blacks. *Black Aging*, 1977, **2**, 17-24.

Nowlin, J. Successful aging: health and social factors in an inter-racial population. *Black Aging*, 1977, **2**, 10-17.

Smith, S. H. The older rural Negro. In Youmans, E. G. (Ed.). *Older rural Americans*. Lexington, Ky.: University of Kentucky Press, 1967, pp. 262-280.

Stone, V. *Personal adjustment in aging in relation to community environment: a study of persons sixty years and over in Carrboro and Chapel Hill, North Carolina*. Unpublished doctoral dissertation, University of North Carolina, Chapel Hill, N.C., 1959.

Walls, B., and Jackson, J. Factors affecting the use of physicians by menopausal black women. *Urban Health*, 1977, **6**, 53-55.

RECOGNITION AND MANAGEMENT OF GRIEF IN ELDERLY PATIENTS

Edwin P. Gramlich, M.D.*

Grief is a ubiquitous bodily reaction to emotional injury and loss, not unlike bodily reactions to physical injury. Known throughout the ages as an important cause of illness, it is diffuse in the aged and obscured, if not completely overlooked, in this age of scientific medicine.[1] If it is not truly a disease, as suggested by Engel,[2] it is certainly a state of disease, with organic and physiologic changes. In its uncomplicated form grief follows a typical and predictable course.[3-7] As with many reactive processes, however, it may follow deviant and atypical courses which are easily confused with other disease processes.[6,8] The more devious patterns of grief are found in the young and the old.[6] It is stated by Nemiah that melancholia is at the bottom of everything, since nothing lasts and all that is loved or shall be loved must die or be lost.[9] Aging, therefore, subjects individuals to more and more loss. Loved ones are lost, health is lost, cherished goals are unrecognized and lost, cherished occupations and sources of pride and value are lost in the progress of time.[4,10,11]

Grief in elderly people has been studied scientifically only on a few occasions[12-15] with contradictory results. Several complete studies of elderly people suggest that grief, as such, may not be a significant event.[15-17] According to the theory of aging proposed by Cummings and Henry, aging people progressively disengage from their environmental attachments and live in an increasingly detached state.[18] It may be, however, that this state is one of a chronic depressive withdrawal and is associated with the continued accumulation of losses and over-

Reproduced from *Geriatrics*, July, 1968, pp. 87-92.
*Straub Clinic, Honolulu, Hawaii.

whelming grief.[1] The recent work of Kastenbaum and Birren supports the general theory that aging is associated with a progressive disengagement from the environment.[15,16] Their theory proposes that grief in itself is not an essentially important factor, but only one of many stresses applied to the aging individual. Other studies, however, have shown that grief is the precipitating factor in many states of illness and tends to aggravate preexisting organic and psychosomatic disorders.[3,10,13,19-21] The death rate of widows and widowers exceeds that of the population by a significant degree, and it is legendary that many have died of, or at least during, grief.[21]

DEFINITION

To understand grief in the elderly patient, one must have a firm understanding of the general syndrome of grief. The grief process is initiated by awareness of a significant loss. The first reaction to the loss is that of shock and disbelief. This state may be intense and associated with hallucinations and delusions in an effort to deny the loss in fantasy. If the loss is denied by the individual a state of numbness prevails.

Usually the loss can be denied only for a short time. It then becomes painfully obvious to the bereaved person that an extremely important other person has died. This initiates a stage of intense physical distress accompanied by feelings of deep loss and emptiness, associated with intense sadness and sorrow. Physical pain is common, especially headache, muscle and joint pain, and pain and pressure in the neck, chest, and abdomen. It is an all encompassing and disorganizing emotional reaction. It tends to come in waves of pain and distress accompanied by weeping.

This stage usually passes to a more chronic stage of mourning associated with a prolonged feeling of depression and sadness and with periodic memories of the lost person. It is debatable whether typical grief carries with it intense feelings of guilt and hostility. Some authors state that it does, others that it does not.[9,23] However, it is common to feel intensely hurt and injured. The intensity of the hurt and injury calls for some explanation and meaning on the part of the grieving person. Intense guilt and self-blame often occur and may be of an entirely irrational nature, depending upon the ambivalence of the relationship with the lost person.

Following the guilt, hostility is common. Friends and family members may be confronted with anger and rejection. Efforts to offer comfort may meet with intense hostility. The person views the world as a hostile place, and projects blame to anyone who comes near. As the grieving person continues to do the work of mourning and to cope with the many memories associated with the lost individual, the process slowly subsides over weeks and months until energy is once again available to invest in new people to replace the lost one. This enables the grieving individual to go on and live a life free from the entanglements of the irretrievable past.

ATYPICAL GRIEF

Atypical grief follows one of three general forms: (1) In delayed grief, the loss may be denied for months or years and grief occurs later, inappropriately associated with a reminder of the loss. This frequently occurs on an anniversary of the loss, the individual having experienced no grief prior to that time. (2) Inhibited grief occurs in individuals in whom mourning seems to be subdued; however, it is longer lasting and associated with disturbed behavior or physical symptoms. It is common in young people. (3) Chronic grief is a prolongation and intensification of the normal grief process. It may be associated with states of overactivity without much sense of loss. It may occur in conditions where the grieving individual has identified with the lost person's illness and has developed symptoms similar to those of that illness. These symptoms may persist. It is as though the lost one has become a part of the grieving individual, who attempts to maintain contact with the deceased through illness, or sympathy pain.

Other patterns of chronic grief have to do with chronic isolation and apathy with depression, chronic hostility with paranoid thinking, and lengthy disorganization of preexisting life patterns. Physical symptomatology is a common part of grief, and chronic grief may be manifested by chronic physical symptoms either due to diagnosable psychosomatic conditions or ill-defined symptoms of pain and dysfunction. Parkes[10] lists osteoarthritis, colitis, migraine, asthma, bronchitis, ulcerative colitis, spastic colon, urticaria, and rheumatoid arthritis as disease entities which may be precipitated or aggravated by a loss.

INHIBITED GRIEF IN THE ELDERLY

Typical grief is thought to be uncommon in aged individuals. More often it follows a pattern of inhibited or chronic grief. The most common manifestation of grief in the aged, therefore, is overt somatic pain and distress. Many aspects of grief do not manifest themselves as clearly and are not as well defined as in younger people. It has been shown that elderly patients, who are grieving, frequently present themselves to physicians with physical complaints. They commonly have gastrointestinal symptoms, or joint and muscular pains, or both.

The most important aspect of the diagnostic process is the preceding history of an important loss, perhaps on its anniversary. One should suspect a grief reaction, regardless of the symptomatology, when one sees an individual who has sustained a major loss within the two years prior to the presenting complaints. Most commonly the physician is consulted within six months of the loss and studies have shown that the incidence of office visits is two to three times as great during the six months following a loss as it was during the six months prior to the loss. Since the grieving process is not experienced as intensely on a conscious level in elderly people, it appears that more of the emotional reaction is suppressed and finds an outlet through somatic expression. Most elderly patients actually hurt rather than complain of emotional pain. In my experience, many grieving elderly people also show symptoms of overt emotional and mental disorder, contrary to some of the literature on the subject. This is particularly evident if one takes the time to inquire about the patient's life after the somatic complaints have been investigated. It is my contention that one cannot rule out the grief process in a symptomatic widow unless there is a definite organic disease to explain the symptomatology. Even then, grief may be a strong contributing factor.

Case report. An 81-year-old Caucasian widow was seen in psychiatric consultation four months after the death of a favorite but very disappointing son. She complained of abdominal discomfort and lack of appetite. She had been constipated and unable to sleep. She was nervous and frequently tearful. As an occupant of a nursing home, she had been overtly and covertly admonished and accused of being a baby because of her tendency to cry copiously. She had, in effect, been told to "shut up and stop grieving," which increased her grief and denied her an outlet. She expressed much guilt over her son's poor history of accomplishment in life. With encouragement to allow her tears to flow freely, she wept for most of one hour and part of another. The nursing staff was encouraged to assist her in her process of grief and to allow her to weep freely. As soon as this was accomplished, the patient's attitude changed markedly and her symptoms subsided. She developed a more optimistic attitude and began to socialize anew with the members of the nursing home. She resumed her cultural role there as a gossip and on follow-up visits showed only little evidence of residual grief. As the anniversary of her husband's death arrived and of her son's approached, she again experienced her symptoms, but with less intensity.

TREATMENT

The management of grief in elderly people must be preceded by recognition and understanding of the underlying process. Once the physician is relatively certain that his patient's symptoms are those of grief the course of action is clear, with few exceptions. In the very old patient who is able to deny the loss and live in a state of unreality free from grief, it might be prudent to avoid challenging the denial. However, in the patient with existing symptoms, denial has been unsuccessful. Here, "grief work" must be at least partly done before the patient can be symptom-free to work toward new human relations and some form of partial engagement with the environment. The term "good grief" conveys the concept that grieving is good, necessary, and therapeutic. "Grief work" consists of remembering the lost individual and of working through the pain, guilt, and anger that go with the memories.[9,23] I encourage grieving patients to cry frequently and to freely share their tears with close members of the family, physicians, nurses, and ministers. Paradoxical intention probably operates here, as many people unconsciously do the opposite of what they are told.

I think it important to share guilt, so that it can be forgiven and its irrational aspects rejected. Those who deal with a grieving patient should accept hostility, not react to it with counterhostility. Sharing of guilt feelings often functions to relieve intolerable guilt and may prevent suicide. Also, if it is understood that the patient is simply venting his anger at being hurt by what seems to be an irrational and unjust world, the anger can be accepted as a natural emotional reaction similar to the inflammatory reaction that naturally follows a burn. An angry reaction from a hurt patient should not be taken personally. A tolerant attitude toward it will help the grieving person accept anger and will keep him from directing it inwardly or suppressing it entirely. As this is accomplished, it is important to encourage the process of resocialization and finding new friends to begin, at least, to substitute for the important lost one. Sometimes the grieving process can interfere with current relationships and it is helpful to explain to friends and relatives that the person's hostility or symptom is a part of grief and will subside if they are patient. New living arrangements may have to be made by family members. Tranquilizing and antidepressant drugs can be used, depending on the target symptoms. They help in subduing emotional reactions and allow the individual to take the grief in smaller doses.

Grieving patients should be told that they are in the process of grief and mourning, for many of them do not connect their pain and misery with their loss. They have worked to deny or avoid memory of the loss, with the idea that not thinking about the loss would make the pain go away. Some say it is silly to cry and it does no good to mourn, not realizing that they only fool the mind. The body and emotional self react anyway as the loss is jerked from the very heart of the being and many wounds are opened that must heal. Many interpret their symptoms as a sign of physical disease or mental illness and need to be repeatedly reassured that the symptoms do not represent those dreaded conditions. A few extra minutes of a physician's time and understanding at this point can be exceedingly helpful to a bereaved patient.

SUMMARY

The process of grief in general, and in the aging patient in particular, is outlined. Grief is viewed as a psychosomatic reaction to an extreme environmental stress that every physician should be cognizant of and alert for, especially in the elderly patient in whom it may be hidden behind a facade of somatic complaints. A program of management and treatment is outlined whereby grief can be shortened and prevented from becoming a more chronic and disabling, if not fatal, disease.

REFERENCES

1. Milt, H.: Grief. Trends in Psychiatry, Vol. 3, No. II. West Point, Pa.: Merck Sharp & Dohme, 1966.
2. Engel, G. L.: Is grief a disease? Psychosom. Med. **23**:18, 1961.
3. Kollar, E. J.: Psychological stress. J. Nerv. Ment. Dis. **132**:382, 1961.
4. Volkan, V.: Normal and pathological grief reactions: A guide of the family physician. Virginia Med. Mth. **93**:651, 1966.
5. Parkes, C. M.: Bereavement and mental illness. Part I. A clinical study of the grief of bereaved psychiatric patients. Brit. J. Med. Psychol. **38**:1, 1965.
6. Parkes, C. M.: Bereavement and mental illness. Brit. J. Med. Psychol. **38**:13, 1965.

7. Lindemann, E.: Symptomatology and management of acute grief. Amer. J. Psychiat. **101:**141, 1944.
8. Engel, G. L.: Grief and grieving. Amer. J. Nursing **64:**93, 1964.
9. Nemiah, J. C.: Foundations of Psychopathology. New York: Oxford: University Press, 1961.
10. Parkes, C. M.: Effects of bereavement on physical and mental health: A study of the medical records of widows. Brit. Med. J. **2:**274, 1964.
11. Schmale, A. H., Jr.: Relationship of separation and depression to disease. Psychosom. Med. **20:**259, 1958.
12. Kay, D. W., Roth, M., and Hopkins, B.: Aetiological factors in the causation of affective disorders in old age. J. Ment. Sci. **101:**302, 1955.
13. Stern, K., Williams, G. M., and Prados, M.: Grief reactions in later life. Amer. J. Psychiat. **108:**289, 1951.
14. Perlin, S., and Butler, R. N.: Human Aging, U.S. Department of Health, Education, and Welfare, National Institute of Mental Health, Bethesda, Md., 1963, p. 159.
15. Birren, J. E., Butler, R. N., Greenhouse, S. W., Sokoloff, L., and Yarrow, M. R.: Human Aging, U.S. Department of Health, Education, and Welfare, National Institute of Mental Health, Bethesda, Md., 1963, p. 314.
16. Kastenbaum, R.: New Thoughts on Old Age. New York: Springer Publishing Co., 1964.
17. Simon, A., and Engle, B.: Geriatrics. Amer. J. Psychiat. **120:**671, 1964.
18. Cummings, E., and Henry, W. E.: Growing Old, New York: Basic Books, 1961.
19. Krupt, G. R.: Identification as a defense against loss. Int. J. Psycho-Anal. **46:**303, 1965.
20. Freud, S.: A General Introduction of Psychoanalysis. New York: Washington Square Press, 1960.
21. Young, M., Benjamin, B., and Wallis, C.: The mortality of widowers. Lancet **2:**454, 1963.
22. Kraus, A. S., and Lilienfeld, A. M.: Some epidemiological aspects of the higher mortality rate in the young widowed group, J. Chron. Dis. **10:**207, 1959.
23. Paul, L.: Crisis intervention. Ment. Hygiene **50:**141, 1966.

12

SUICIDE AND AGING

H. L. P. Resnik, M.D.,* and Joel M. Cantor, Ph.D.**

The Bureau of Census has estimated that in the year 1970, 20 million persons living in the United States will be aged 65 or over, and because of increasing longevity due to medical advances, there will be 25 million in the year 1985. How many of them will die prematurely by suicide? And, more important, how many will have "died" years before actual physical death?

Suicide causes about 1 per cent of the deaths reported each year; in 1967 that meant about 23,000. The suicide rate has averaged 11 per 100,000 since 1900 for the entire population, but different rates are reported for different groups.[14]

White males over 65 commit suicide three times more often than do white males aged 20-24, and their suicide rate is four times greater than the overall rate for the United States. White females over 65 commit suicide twice as often as white females aged 20-24, although the highest rate occurs earlier, between the ages of 45 and 54. Because at present the recording and reporting of suicide is often incomplete for nonwhites, it is difficult to discern any particular pattern of change for blacks (or nonwhites inclusively). However, the black suicide rate virtually equals the white rate until age 35, when the white rate becomes two to three times higher than the black. Factoring of our urban-rural statistics would probably show that the suicide rate among black adolescents may be higher than among whites living in metropolitan areas. As this young group of nonwhites ages, the reported incidence of suicide among them may be significantly higher.

Marital status seems to influence suicide rates. They are lower for the married

Reproduced from *Journal of the American Geriatrics Society*, February, 1970, **18**,152-158.
Presented at the National Conference of Social Workers, New York City, May 27, 1969.
*Chief, Center for Studies of Suicide Prevention (Room 12A-01), National Institute of Mental Health, 5454 Wisconsin Avenue, Chevy Chase, Maryland 20015.
**Consultant in Program Development, Center for Studies of Suicide Prevention.

and higher for those living alone, through choice or the death of a spouse—a factor not to be ignored in our older population.

Suicide is currently listed among the ten leading causes of death, but more careful and realistic recording might show it to be even more common. Certainly, in most age groups (including the aged), many suicides are concealed in the data for accidents and natural deaths.[15]

Since 1950, there has been a noticeable decline in suicide for those over age 65. The rate of white males aged 65-74 has dropped 26 per cent, and for white females aged 75-84, 25 per cent. There has been a similar decline in England, Norway and Denmark. Farber[2] is of the opinion that the introduction of social security plans reduces suicide potential in the aged by relieving economic distress. We believe this to be only one of a number of variables involved. However, we are concerned here with the increase in the absolute numbers of the aged and the total number of suicides. The aged comprise 9 per cent of the population, yet they contribute 25 per cent of the suicides.

THEORETICAL CONSIDERATIONS

Modern Western psychodynamic thinking about suicide began in the early 1900's with Freud's theory that the unconscious influences man's everyday behavior. He saw two opposing forces at work: an instinct for death, Thanatos, and an instinct for life, Eros. Menninger, writing in 1931 ("Man Against Himself"), broadened the concept of the death instinct and pointed out that man as easily turns his aggression inward as outward, and can use numerous self-destructive opportunities to kill himself. He cited as examples excessive drinking, smoking and auto racing. One might add neglect of one's physical condition, frequent accidents (including automobile accidents) and other risk-taking behavior. Menninger suggested that we think of such behavior as a form of "partial" or "chronic" suicide. He also identified three aspects of the suicide act as manifestations of the death instinct: the wish to kill, to be killed, and to die. When a suicide occurs, the person killed is one who was once loved, then internalized, and then hated. Murder of the hated person results in one's own death. The wish to be killed can be understood as stemming from the guilt associated with the hate, and the person's need to be punished.[3,5] Concepts about death and dying are always relevant when dealing with suicidal persons.

Jung also contributed to our understanding of suicide by suggesting that a person who commits suicide might wish for a rebirth into a more meaningful and spiritual existence. This is a not uncommon wish of older people. Hendin deals with suicide as a dependency conflict, seeing some suicides as acts of retaliation for real or imagined abandonment. "You abandoned me! Now I will abandon you!" Abandonment is very real for many aged people. Horney was one of the first of the psychoanalysts to consider social factors as an influence. Thus suicide could occur when the person was in a state of extreme self-alienation. This can be a realistic reaction to the rejection felt by so many of the aged.[6]

The sociological study of suicide began with the publication of Durkheim's *Le Suicide* in 1897. He had noticed that different suicide rates for various countries and groups remained stable over long periods, and wondered whether such differences might be due to differences in group cohesion. If so, suicide rates might be used as an index of social organization. He also classified suicides into three types: the altruistic (rarely seen with the aged), the egoistic, and the anomic. Maris[8] recently has pointed out that such a classification cannot be considered adequate without the dimension of intrapsychic conflict being correlated with the sociological.

Egoistic suicide occurs in persons living outside of a group, because they are not subject to group inhibitions about suicide and also are deprived of the kind of emotional support available in group membership. Suicide in the aging may be seen as "egoistic" in Durkheim's sense, because the gradual loosening of group ties is a part of the aging process in Western society.

Anomie connotes "normalessness" or absence of group rules regulating conduct. Anomie becomes more of a problem during periods of rapid social change because people become confused as to what is appropriate or proper conduct. Older persons, who often need clearcut guidelines to feel "good" or "safe," may become acutely anxious and disorganized when these guidelines are not present. This factor may well increase suicide in the aged, as our society has not provided identifiable norms for the behavior of older persons.

INDICATORS OF SUICIDAL POTENTIAL

Some indicators of higher suicide potential, as described by Litman and Farberow,[7] may be applied to aged persons. These variables all contribute toward evaluation of a subject's lethality potential, i.e., the probability for a successful suicide.

Prior suicidal behavior. Various surveys show that 1 in 3 suicide attempters eventually kills himself, and that 1 in 3 completers has a history of prior attempts. Gardner et al.[4] found that, in persons with suicidal histories, suicide occurs nine times more often in those under 55, and eighteen times more often in those over 55. Research findings indicate that aged persons have fewer histories of prior attempts and are also less likely to "cry for help." But when the aged do cry for help, we should heed the communication, as they are much more likely to make an attempt with a more lethal method, and thus be more successful.

Bereavement and loss. Suicide potential is heightened when there has been recent or recurrent loss of loved ones. Moss and Hamilton[10] noted that among the aged, the loss or death of close relatives occurred twice as often for a group of suicide attempters as for a control group. Since loss of relatives and friends as one ages is unavoidable, new relationships must constantly be substituted. As Rachlis[11] has pointed out, the most common losses are of mates, jobs, earnings, physical health and mobility, mental health, life expectancy and status. How many of us can tolerate *one* or more of these insults, especially when we are unable to undo them? Mourning and bereavement become essential problems for the gerontologist, and a comfortable attitude toward them is an essential skill.

Psychiatric disorders. Numerous studies indicate that suicidal behavior occurs more frequently when there is a history of organic brain disease, especially if accompanied by depressive affect. The findings of Gardner et al.[4] in Monroe County, New York show the increasing risk of suicide with psychiatric illness.

Serious physical illness. Serious and chronic health problems causing economic and physical distress may also be an important factor. Frequent exacerbations of chronic illness may increase suicidal potential.

Dorpat et al.[1] studied suicide in patients over the age of 60 and found that 85 per cent of them had an active serious physical illness at the time of death. Apparently, in the aged, the presence of such illness exacerbates the fear of dying, and some of these patients may prefer to precipitate death rather than wait for it passively.

Putting effects in order. Examples of this would be updating a will, changing the beneficiaries of an insurance policy, or giving personal possessions to friends. The victim's behavior not only indicates preparation and planning for death, but might even predate the death by carrying out what usually would be the responsibility of surviving relatives and friends. Putting effects in order, however, may be appropriate and mature. This behavior must be evaluated as one of a constellation of many variables.

Suicidal threats. It is not true, as popularly believed, that those who "talk about it won't do it." Surveys show that high percentages of threateners become attempters, and attempters become completers. In the aged, *all* threats or attempts *must* be taken seriously. The likelihood of a success is many times higher than in other groups. One must be especially careful when the threat is specific about the time, place and method.

THERAPEUTIC INTERVENTION

The identification and diagnosis of self-destructive activity is far from even approaching an exact science. Nevertheless, there are some guidelines, as just described. These are based primarily on clinical experience. Current research is aimed at examining these concepts more rigorously.

Mintz[9] has recently outlined the most comprehensive treatment approach.

Treatment is a more serious problem than identification. Patients may be either acutely or chronically suicidal. Whereas crisis intervention on an extremely personal level may suffice for the former, other techniques must be developed for the latter. A depressed aged person is a difficult client. All too often there is pressure for hospital admission, and this may be the best way for a family or a therapist to be rid of ongoing responsibility. We need not remind you that suicidal people kill themselves in hospitals.

Taking action. The first step must be to establish trust. When a suicidal person has given up with regard to his own ability to solve his problems and when the clues to his suicidal intent have been ignored, he may also stop believing that others are interested in helping him. There is more here than simply establishing confidence in a technical ability to help; there must be a demonstration that the patient will be handled with sincerity, warmth and concern. It should not be forgotten that suicide is still taboo to many people.

Once the crisis is understood, it is important that the therapist *act*. Any appropriate realistic step he takes to improve the impasse that overwhelms the victim may lift the feelings of hopelessness and despair. "Taking action" may be no more than a promise of help. It is important also that the therapist be decisive and authoritative because of the confusion and ambivalence felt by the patient. Because the patient's own judgment can no longer be trusted, the therapist must instill confidence that he knows what needs to be done, and will do it. When a life is at stake, the therapist should, if necessary, act *as if* he were omnipotent.

Involving others. The therapist's role as a professional who evaluates the situation and starts a therapeutic and rehabilitative attack on the underlying problem is not enough. He not only must provide the temporary and short-term therapeutic support needed until the emergency subsides, but he must be available for a continued relationship. It is also essential to recruit "significant others" who can help turn the patient back toward life, after they are instructed in the seriousness of the situation, and made responsible for continuing the recovery process. It is bad professional handling to conceal a potential suicide, and it is dangerous for the future of the attempter.

The best therapeutic approach is to have concerned relatives and friends gather to assist and comfort the patient, since this re-establishes the social ties which may have been severed. Too many suicidal and depressed patients are an occupational hazard. The burden should be shared with colleagues, friends and spouse, within professional limits.

In the case of the aged, however, prevention may have to precede intervention immediately before an actual attempt at suicide. Because "normal" aging in Western society is a gradual phasing-out and reduction of activity, the older person can plan and effect an earlier death than necessary, without detection. Numerous self-destructive behaviors and opportunities are available to the older person, e.g., deliberate self-starvation, balking at medically prescribed self-care, hazardous activities, or voluntary seclusion. Any older person living alone, who has lost his self-respect and his group-identity, who has financial difficulty, and who is worried over chronic illness and afraid of tomorrow, is a high risk for suicide.

New techniques must be developed for the case-finding of suicidal persons, especially older ones. Several such techniques include befriending or the "buddy system" of calls or visits, the employment of elderly persons by suicide prevention centers as telephone answerers and as speakers on suicide prevention, and the use of senior-citizen centers for the early identification of suicidal older persons by direct case finding. For instance, try asking the next 100 aged persons,

"Have you, in the past, or recently, thought of ending it all?" You won't precipitate an attempt.

There is a growing awareness that the fear of an "old age" death may paradoxically lead an older person to a self-induced, premature death for the purpose of escaping it all. It is also possible that an older person may want to die because he feels that others want him to die.

Here we introduce the concept of self-determined (we have not said suicidal) death for the aged. It is conceivable that as our aged population increases and as our medical and nursing facilities continuously fail to meet the needs, certain selected patients, informed of a fatal illness and prognosis, may be given the privilege and means of ending their own lives. The aged in some cultures and species do this.

The National Center for Studies of Suicide Prevention has allocated a high priority to self-destructive behaviors in the aged and we hope that those who work with this high-risk group will become interested in investigating the problem in depth. There is an unfortunate shortage of skilled mental-health professionals who have a specific interest in treating the dying, the self-destructive and the suicidal, especially when these are old people who may be less useful, less resourceful and less accommodating than younger people.

REFERENCES

1. Dorpat, T. L.; Anderson, W. F., and Ripley, H. S.: The relationship of physical illness to suicide, in Suicidal Behaviors: Diagnosis and Management, ed. by H. L. P. Resnik. Boston; Little, Brown and Co., 1968.
2. Farber, M. L.: Suicide and the welfare state, Ment. Hyg. **49:**371-373, 1965.
3. Fenichel, O.: The Psychoanalytic Theory of Neurosis. New York, Norton, 1945.
4. Gardner, E. A.; Bahn, A. K., and Mack, M.: Suicide and psychiatric care in the aging, Arch. Gen. Psychiat. **10:**547-553, 1964.
5. Jackson, D. D.: Theories of suicide, in Clues to Suicide, ed. by E. S. Shneidman and N. L. Farberow. New York, McGraw-Hill, 1957.
6. Kastenbaum, R.: Multiple perspectives on a geriatric "death valley," Comm. Ment. Health J. **3:**21-29, 1967.
7. Litman, R. E., and Farberow, N. L.: Emergency evaluation of self-destructive potentiality, in The Cry for Help, ed. by N. L. Farberow and E. S. Shneidman. New York, McGraw-Hill, 1961.
8. Maris, R. W.: Social Forces in Urban Suicide. Homewood, Ill., Dorsey Press, 1969.
9. Mintz, R. S.: Psychotherapy of the suicidal patient, in Suicidal Behaviors: Diagnosis and Management, ed. by H. L. P. Resnik. Boston; Little, Brown and Co., 1968.
10. Moss, L. M., and Hamilton, D. M.: Psychotherapy of the suicidal patient, Am. J. Psychiat. **112:**814-820, 1956.
11. Rachlis, D.: Suicide and loss adjustment in the aging. Presented at Second Annual Conference, American Association of Suicidology, New York City, March 30, 1969.
12. Walker, D. W.: A study of the relationship between suicide rate and age in the U.S. (1914 to 1964). Program, Annual Meeting, American Statistical Assn., Washington, D.C., 1967.
13. Weiss, J. M. A.: Suicide in the aged, in Suicidal Behaviors: Diagnosis and Management, ed. by H. L. P. Resnik. Boston; Little, Brown and Co., 1968.
14. National Center for Health Statistics: Vital Statistics of the United States. Washington, D.C., Govt. Printing Office.
15. National Center for Health Statistics: Suicide in the United States, 1950-1964. PHS Publication No. 1000, Series 20, No. 5., Washington, D.C., Govt. Printing Office, August 1967.